T O U

TouchPoints
for Men

GOD'S ANSWERS FOR

YOUR DAILY NEEDS

Tyndale House Publishers, Inc.
Wheaton, Illinois

Visit Tyndale's exciting Web site at www.tyndale.com

Copyright © 1996, 1998 by Tyndale House Publishers, Inc. All rights
reserved.

Notes and special features copyright © 1996, 1998 by V. Gilbert Beers
and Ronald A. Beers. All rights reserved.

General Editors: V. Gilbert Beers and Ronald A. Beers

Scripture selection and note writing primarily by Shawn A. Harrison.

Tyndale House Editor: Shawn A. Harrison

Portions of this book compiled from *The TouchPoint Bible*, copyright
© 1996 by Tyndale House Publishers.

Scripture quotations are taken from the *Holy Bible*, New Living
Translation, copyright © 1996. Used by permission of Tyndale House
Publishers, Inc., Wheaton, Illinois 60189. All rights reserved.

New Living and the New Living Translation logo are registered
trademarks of Tyndale House Publishers, Inc.

ISBN 0-8423-3307-X

Printed in the United States of America

05   04   03   02   01   00   99   98
10   9   8   7   6   5   4   3   2   1

ABSENCE

Why does it sometimes seem that God is absent?

Psalm 10:1 *O LORD, why do you stand so far away? Why do you hide when I need you the most?*
The greater our troubles, the farther away God sometimes seems.

Psalm 139:2, 7 *You know when I sit down or stand up. You know my every thought. . . . I can never escape from your spirit! I can never get away from your presence!*
Even though we may feel that God is far away, he is in fact very near to us at all times.

Isaiah 59:1-2 *Listen! The LORD . . . can hear you when you call. But there is a problem—your sins have cut you off from God.*

1

Sin is a wall that separates us from God. Sometimes we miss the joy of fellowship with God because of our sin.

James 4:7-8 Humble yourselves before God. . . . Draw close to God, and God will draw close to you. If we want to have restored fellowship with God, we need to have a humble attitude, confess our sins, and draw near to God. Humility puts us in sync with Jesus.

Why is it important for us not to be absent (from our families, from our jobs, from the church, etc.)?

Genesis 37:18-29 When Joseph's brothers saw him coming, they recognized him in the distance and made plans to kill him. . . . "Come on, let's kill him and throw him into a deep pit. . . . " But Reuben came to Joseph's rescue. . . . Reuben was secretly planning to help Joseph escape. . . . When [a group of traders] came by, his brothers pulled Joseph out of the pit and sold him. . . . Some time later, Reuben returned to get Joseph out of the pit. When he discovered that Joseph was missing, he tore his clothes in anguish and frustration.

When we are absent, we miss crucial events in the lives of others. We can do much good with our presence, but things can go very badly in our absence.

Matthew 25:10 *While they were gone to buy oil, the bridegroom came, and those who were ready went in with him to the marriage feast, and the door was locked.* When we are absent, we miss important opportunities.

Hebrews 10:25 *Let us not neglect our meeting together, as some people do, but encourage and warn each other, especially now that the day of his coming back again is drawing near.* Neglecting church may cause us to neglect God.

Are there times when it is best for us to be absent?

Genesis 27:41-42 *Esau hated Jacob . . . and he said to himself, "My father will soon be dead and gone. Then I will kill Jacob." But . . . Rebekah . . . sent for Jacob and told him, "Esau is threatening to kill you. . . . Flee to your uncle Laban in Haran."* Sometimes discretion requires absence from an inflamed situation. (Also see 1 Sam. 19:11-12.)

2 Samuel 11:6-11 *David . . . told Uriah, "Go on home and relax." . . . But Uriah wouldn't go home. . . . [He] replied, "The Ark and the armies of Israel and Judah are living in tents, and Joab and his officers are camping in the open fields. How could I go home to wine and dine and sleep with my wife? I swear that I will never be guilty of acting like that."*

There may be times in our lives that a higher duty calls for our absence from our families and homes.

What should we do when we cannot avoid our own or another's absence?

1 Samuel 13:8 *Saul waited there seven days for Samuel, as Samuel had instructed him earlier, but Samuel still didn't come. . . . So he demanded, "Bring me the burnt offering and the peace offerings!" And Saul sacrificed the burnt offering himself.*

When others are absent, we should still be obedient to God and trust.

1 Thessalonians 2:17 *Dear brothers and sisters, after we were separated from you for a little while (though our hearts never left you), we tried very hard to come back because of our intense longing to see you again.*

When we are away from our families, we should keep in touch with them as much as possible, praying for them along the way and looking forward to our reunion.

PROMISE FROM GOD: Matthew 28:20 *Be sure of this: I am with you always, even to the end of the age.*

Accomplishments

What is our greatest accomplishment? How do we achieve it?

Romans 1:17 *This Good News tells us how God makes us right in his sight. This is accomplished from start to finish by faith. As the Scriptures say, "It is through faith that a righteous person has life."*

Salvation, the greatest of accomplishments, is not the work of our hands, but the work of God in our hearts.

Ecclesiastes 12:13 *Here is my final conclusion: Fear God and obey his commands, for this is the duty of every person.*

Obeying God is life's greatest accomplishment.

How can I do a better job of accomplishing things?

Isaiah 25:1 *O LORD, I will honor and praise your name, for you are my God. You do such wonderful things! You planned them long ago, and now you have accomplished them.*

Accomplishments come with good planning. God planned before he accomplished, a good model for us to follow.

How can I get more done?

Ecclesiastes 4:9 *Two people can accomplish more than twice as much as one; they get a better return for their labor.*

Accomplishments are multiplied through teamwork. It is impossible for one person to play a duet or trio. It is hard to win a football or soccer game without a team. It is hard to have a happy marriage if only one mate works at it. How encouraging to note that two people can actually do more than twice as much as one, as long as they are pulling in the same direction.

Is it wrong to be proud of our accomplishments?

1 Corinthians 4:7 *What makes you better than anyone else? What do you have that God hasn't given you? And if all you have is from God, why boast as though you have accomplished something on your own?*

There is a healthy satisfaction of accomplishment that includes thanksgiving to God for what he has done through us. But it is arrogance to think the deed was done all by ourselves.

PROMISE FROM GOD: Psalm 60:12 *With God's help we will do mighty things.*

ACCOUNTABILITY

How do I become more accountable?

Psalm 1:1 *Oh, the joys of those who do not follow the advice of the wicked.*

Proverbs 27:6 *Wounds from a friend are better than many kisses from an enemy.*

To become more accountable, follow God's commands as outlined in his Word, the Bible. And choose wise friends to whom you can feel free to give an account of yourself.

What happens when there is no accountability?

Judges 17:6 *The people did whatever seemed right in their own eyes.*

1 Samuel 13:11-13 *Saul replied, ". . . You didn't arrive when you said you would. . . . I felt obliged to offer the burnt offering myself."*

Left unaccountable, we will always lean toward sin, and the consequences of those sins will hurt not only us but many others, including God.

How can I effectively hold someone else accountable?

Exodus 18:21-22 *Find some capable, honest men who fear God and hate bribes. . . . They will help you carry the load, making the task easier for you.*

Titus 1:6-8 *He must not be arrogant or quick-tempered. . . . He must live wisely and be fair. He must live a devout and disciplined life.*
If we are going to minister to others by holding them accountable, we must be wise, honest, godly, and trustworthy.

Is it really important for others to help us be accountable?

Proverbs 12:15 *Fools think they need no advice, but the wise listen to others.*
Good advisers keep us from actions that can hurt us.

PROMISE FROM GOD: 1 John 2:3 *How can we be sure we belong to him? By obeying his commandments.*

ADULTERY

What is God's definition of adultery?

Hebrews 13:4 *Give honor to marriage, and remain faithful to one another in marriage. God will surely judge people who are immoral and those who commit adultery.*
Adultery is being unfaithful to your mate. Normally, this involves forming a sexual relationship with someone other than your spouse. But even an intimate emotional relationship with another can

become adulterous if it takes us away from our first love. Similarly, in the spiritual realm, we commit adultery against God when we are unfaithful to him by worshiping anything except him. (*See* IDOLATRY.)

Mark 10:11 *He told them, "Whoever divorces his wife and marries someone else commits adultery against her."*
The commitment to remain faithful "until death do us part" is a serious commitment and should not be taken lightly.

Matthew 5:28 *Anyone who even looks at a woman with lust in his eye has already committed adultery with her in his heart.*
When we look at another woman with lust, we are being unfaithful to our wives.

Why is it important for us not to get involved in adultery?

Exodus 20:14 *Do not commit adultery.*
God has commanded us to be faithful to our wives.

Proverbs 6:27-29 *Can a man scoop fire into his lap and not be burned? Can he walk on hot coals and not blister his feet? So it is with the man who sleeps with another man's wife. He who embraces her will not go unpunished.*

A moment's pleasure in adultery just isn't worth the consequences that it brings—a lifetime of regret and pain.

1 Corinthians 6:9-10 *Don't you know that those who do wrong will have no share in the Kingdom of God? . . . Those who indulge in sexual sin, who are . . . adulterers . . . none of these will have a share in the Kingdom of God.*
Even if we are not caught in our sin during our lifetime, we won't get away with it forever.

How do we protect ourselves from getting into an adulterous relationship?

Proverbs 2:16 *Wisdom will save you from the immoral woman, from the flattery of the adulterous woman.*
God promises wisdom to those who ask him for it (James 1:5). When we have wisdom, we will know how to avoid getting into adultery.

Proverbs 4:25-27 *Look straight ahead, and fix your eyes on what lies before you. Mark out a straight path for your feet; then stick to the path and stay safe. Don't get sidetracked; keep your feet from following evil.*
If looking at other women can lead us into adultery, then keeping our eyes off of them will help us to stay away from it. It can be challenging to have "faithful eyes," but it is a key to our success in avoiding adultery.

Proverbs 5:3-9 *The lips of an immoral woman are as sweet as honey, and her mouth is smoother than oil. But the result is as bitter as poison, sharp as a double-edged sword. . . . So now, my sons, listen to me. Never stray from what I am about to say: Run from her! Don't go near the door of her house! If you do, you will lose your honor and hand over to merciless people everything you have achieved in life.*
When faced with temptation, we might be tempted to think that we can "handle it," but the best course is to *run away,* like Joseph did, and not look back!

Proverbs 5:15, 18 *Drink water from your own well—share your love only with your wife. . . . Let your wife be a fountain of blessing for you. Rejoice in the wife of your youth.*
Adultery is only possible if we allow discontentment to creep into our hearts. But we can be content and satisfied with our mate. Then we won't "shop around."

PROMISE FROM GOD: Proverbs 6:24 *These commands and this teaching will keep you from the immoral woman, from the smooth tongue of an adulterous woman.*

Matthew 5:8 *God blesses those whose hearts are pure, for they will see God.*

11

AMBITION

What kinds of ambitions does God want us to have?

Psalm 27:4 *The one thing I ask of the LORD—the thing I seek most—is to live in the house of the LORD all the days of my life, delighting in the LORD's perfections and meditating in his Temple.*

Having a relationship with God and fellowship with him should be the highest aspiration of our lives.

Matthew 5:6, 9 *God blesses those who are hungry and thirsty for justice, for they will receive it in full. . . . God blesses those who work for peace, for they will be called the children of God.*

1 Corinthians 14:1 *Let love be your highest goal.*

Matthew 28:19-20 *Go and make disciples of all the nations. . . . Teach these new disciples to obey all the commands I have given you.*

We should focus on achieving such things as justice, peace, and love in the world and on bringing people into fellowship with God.

What are the right ways for us to pursue our ambitions?

Isaiah 58:13 *Honor the LORD in everything you do, and don't follow your own desires.*

12

Matthew 23:11-12 *The greatest among you must be a servant. But those who exalt themselves will be humbled, and those who humble themselves will be exalted.*
Honor God in your goals, and he will honor you in your accomplishments.

1 Corinthians 9:26 *So I run straight to the goal with purpose in every step. I am not like a boxer who misses his punches.*

Colossians 4:5 *Make the most of every opportunity.*
If we are going to achieve the ambitions that God has given us, we must be focused on our goal and take every opportunity.

What kinds of ambitions are harmful?

Matthew 4:8-10 *"I will give it all to you,"* [Satan] said, *"if you will only kneel down and worship me." "Get out of here, Satan," Jesus told him. "For the Scriptures say, 'You must worship the Lord your God; serve only him.'"*

Matthew 16:24 *Jesus said to the disciples, "If any of you wants to be my follower, you must put aside your selfish ambition, shoulder your cross, and follow me."*
We must never sacrifice our faithfulness and devotion to God in order to pursue our ambitions.

Genesis 11:4 *Let's build a great city with a tower that reaches to the skies—a monument to our greatness! This will bring us together and keep us from scattering all over the world.*
Working to glorify ourselves is an ambition that never pleases God.

Habakkuk 2:9, 12 *How terrible it will be for you who get rich by unjust means! . . . How terrible it will be for you who build cities with money gained by murder and corruption!*
If we work for wealth at the expense of other people's welfare, we will experience God's judgment.

James 4:2 *You want what you don't have, so you scheme and kill to get it. You are jealous for what others have, and you can't possess it, so you fight and quarrel to take it away from them.*
Ambition that is fueled by discontent and a desire for more almost always results in our dishonoring God with our lives.

PROMISE FROM GOD: Psalm 37:4 *Take delight in the LORD, and he will give you your heart's desires.*

ANGER

Why do we usually get angry?

Numbers 22:29 *"Because you have made me look like a fool!" Balaam shouted.*
We get angry when our pride is hurt.

Genesis 4:4-5 *The LORD accepted Abel's offering, but he did not accept Cain's. This made Cain very angry and dejected.*
We get angry when someone else is acknowledged instead of us.

2 Chronicles 26:18-19 *"Get out of the sanctuary, for you have sinned. . . ." Uzziah was furious and refused to set down the incense burner he was holding.*

Esther 3:2-5 *Mordecai refused to bow down or show [Haman] respect. . . . [Haman] was filled with rage.*
We get angry when we don't get our way.

1 Samuel 18:8 *This made Saul very angry. "What's this?" he said. "They credit David with ten thousands and me with only thousands."*
We get angry when we become jealous of what others have or have done.

1 Kings 22:18-27 *"Didn't I tell you," the king of Israel said. . . . "He never prophesies anything but bad news for me. . . . Put this man in prison, and feed him nothing but bread and water."*
We get angry when we are confronted about our sinful actions.

When is it OK to be angry?

John 2:15-16 *[Jesus] drove out the sheep and oxen, scattered the money changers' coins . . . and . . . told them, "Get these things out of here. Don't turn my Father's house into a marketplace!"*

Numbers 25:10-11 *Phinehas . . . has turned my anger away from the Israelites by displaying passionate zeal among them on my behalf.*
Anger at sin is not only appropriate but necessary.

When we are angry, what should we avoid?

James 3:5 *The tongue is a small thing, but what enormous damage it can do.*
Avoid speaking your mind when you are angry. You may say something you will regret.

1 Samuel 19:9-10 *As David played his harp for the king, Saul hurled his spear at David in an attempt to kill him.*
Avoid acting on impulse in the heat of anger. You may do something you will regret.

We all get angry at times, so what should we do about it?

Ephesians 4:26 *"Don't sin by letting anger gain control over you." Don't let the sun go down while you are still angry, for anger gives a mighty foothold to the Devil.*

Stay under the control of the Holy Spirit through prayer, and try to resolve your anger quickly.

PROMISE FROM GOD: Psalm 103:8 *The LORD is merciful and gracious; he is slow to get angry and full of unfailing love.*

APPROVAL

Do we have to earn God's approval?

Galatians 2:19 *When I tried to keep the law, I realized I could never earn God's approval.*

Romans 8:39 *Nothing in all creation will ever be able to separate us from the love of God that is revealed in Christ Jesus our Lord.*

We cannot earn God's approval; instead, he freely gives it to us.

If God's approval is not earned, how can we receive it?

Hebrews 11:5 *It was by faith that Enoch was taken up to heaven without dying—"suddenly he disappeared because God took him." But before he was taken up, he was approved as pleasing to God.*

John 3:16 *God so loved the world that he gave his only Son, so that everyone who believes in him will not perish but have eternal life.*

We receive God's approval by believing that Jesus Christ is God's only Son, and that Jesus died on the cross for our sins so that we could have eternal life in heaven with him. There is nothing else we need to do!

How should we give our approval to others?

Romans 12:9-10 *Don't just pretend that you love others. Really love them. Hate what is wrong. Stand on the side of the good. Love each other with genuine affection, and take delight in honoring each other.*

Loving and serving others affirms their value and worth as creations of God.

What are the things we should not approve of?

Romans 13:13 *We should be decent and true in everything we do, so that everyone can approve of our behavior. Don't participate in wild parties and getting drunk, or in adultery and immoral living, or in fighting and jealousy.*

We should not approve of anything that contradicts God's word.

PROMISE FROM GOD: Romans 15:7 *So accept each other just as Christ has accepted you; then God will be glorified.*

ATTITUDE

What kind of attitude does God want us to have?

1 Corinthians 13:4-7 *Love is patient and kind. Love is not jealous or boastful or proud or rude. Love does not demand its own way. Love is not irritable, and it keeps no record of when it has been wronged. It is never glad about injustice but rejoices whenever the truth wins out. Love never gives up, never loses faith, is always hopeful, and endures through every circumstance.*

An attitude of love sums up many aspects of a good attitude toward others.

Philippians 2:5-8 *Your attitude should be the same that Christ Jesus had. . . . He made himself nothing; he took the humble position of a slave. . . . And in human form he obediently humbled himself even further by dying a criminal's death on a cross.* An attitude of humility and of serving other people will help us to be more like Christ.

Philippians 4:4-6 *Always be full of joy in the Lord. I say it again—rejoice! . . . Don't worry about anything; instead, pray about everything. Tell God what you need, and thank him for all he has done.* An attitude of faith in God has many positive aspects: joy in every circumstance, dependence on God in prayer rather than worrying, and thankfulness—no matter what.

What kind of attitude is displeasing to God?

Genesis 4:6-7 *"Why are you so angry?"* the LORD asked him. *"Why do you look so dejected? You will be accepted if you respond in the right way. But if you refuse to respond correctly, then watch out! Sin is waiting to attack and destroy you, and you must subdue it."* Responding with resentment to God's discipline can lead us into sin.

Numbers 21:5 *"Why have you brought us out of Egypt to die here in the wilderness?" they complained. "There is nothing to eat here and nothing to drink. And we hate this wretched manna!"*
Complaining shows a lack of appreciation for what God has given us.

Proverbs 18:12 *Haughtiness goes before destruction.*
Relying on our own greatness rather than God's greatness leads to self-destruction.

What is the key to having a good attitude?

Romans 8:6 *If your sinful nature controls your mind, there is death. But if the Holy Spirit controls your mind, there is life and peace.*
Letting God's Holy Spirit control our minds, rather than letting our sinful nature control it, is the key to having a good attitude.

Romans 12:2 *Don't copy the behavior and customs of this world, but let God transform you into a new person by changing the way you think.*
When we give God control over our lives, he gives us his attitudes and his ways.

PROMISE FROM GOD: Matthew
5:3-8 *God blesses those who realize their need for
him, for the Kingdom of Heaven is given to them. . . .
God blesses those who are gentle and lowly, for the
whole earth will belong to them. . . . God blesses
those whose hearts are pure, for they will see God.*

AUTHORITY

Why is human authority necessary?

Judges 21:25 *In those days Israel had no king, so
the people did whatever seemed right in their own
eyes.*

1 Peter 2:13-14 *For the Lord's sake, accept all
authority—the king as head of state, and the officials
he has appointed. For the king has sent them to
punish all who do wrong and to honor those who do
right.*
God has appointed human authorities to uphold
and enforce his laws in society.

Should I submit to the authority of the government?

Romans 13:1-2 *Obey the government, for God is
the one who put it there. All governments have been
placed in power by God. So those who refuse to obey
the laws of the land are refusing to obey God, and
punishment will follow.*

God wants us to obey the authorities, which he has appointed to govern our lives.

Acts 4:19; 5:29 *But Peter and John replied, "Do you think God wants us to obey you rather than him? . . . We must obey God rather than human authority."*
Sometimes we must disobey human authorities who tell us to disobey God; God is the higher authority, and we must obey him first.

What is the ultimate source of authority?

John 19:11 *Jesus said, "You would have no power over me at all unless it were given to you from above."*
God is the ultimate source of authority over people's lives and over governments.

Exodus 20:2 *I am the LORD your God, who rescued you from slavery in Egypt.*
In a special way, God is the ultimate authority over his chosen people because he has bought them out of slavery.

2 Timothy 3:16 *All Scripture is inspired by God and is useful to teach us what is true and to make us realize what is wrong in our lives. It straightens us out and teaches us to do what is right.*
Because Scripture comes from the mouth of God, it has ultimate authority over our lives.

What kind of authority does Jesus have?

Matthew 28:18 *Jesus came and told his disciples, "I have been given complete authority in heaven and on earth."*

God has given Jesus authority over everything and everyone in the universe.

Colossians 1:15-18 *Christ is the visible image of the invisible God. He . . . is supreme over all creation. . . . Everything has been created through him and for him. . . . Christ is the head of the church, which is his body.*

Christ, as God, has all of the authority that God has, including authority over the lives of his chosen people.

PROMISE FROM GOD: John 17:2 *You have given him authority over everyone in all the earth. He gives eternal life to each one you have given him.*

Revelation 11:15 *The whole world has now become the Kingdom of our Lord and of his Christ, and he will reign forever and ever.*

BALANCE

How do I live a balanced life?

Romans 13:14 *Let the Lord Jesus Christ take control of you, and don't think of ways to indulge your evil desires.*

Romans 8:6 *If your sinful nature controls your mind, there is death. But if the Holy Spirit controls your mind, there is life and peace.*

When we let Christ have control of our lives, he will help us to bring everything into balance, giving us life and peace.

Psalm 37:34 *Don't be impatient for the LORD to act! Travel steadily along his path.*

Trusting God in everything helps us to keep our lives in balance.

Proverbs 12:3 *Wickedness never brings stability; only the godly have deep roots.*

Living a godly life in harmony with God's will gives us the stability we long for.

Luke 3:14 *"What should we do?" asked some soldiers. John replied, "Don't extort money. . . . And be content with your pay."*

25

1 Timothy 6:6-9 *True religion with contentment is great wealth. . . . So if we have enough food and clothing, let us be content. But people who long to be rich fall into temptation and are trapped by many foolish and harmful desires that plunge them into ruin and destruction.*

Hebrews 13:5 *Be satisfied with what you have.* Often imbalance comes into our lives when we become discontented with what we have. Contentment gives us freedom.

1 Corinthians 9:26-27 *I run straight to the goal with purpose in every step. I am not like a boxer who misses his punches. I discipline my body like an athlete, training it to do what it should.*
When we fully understand what work God has given us to do, we can focus on that and remove distractions that throw our lives out of balance.

PROMISE FROM GOD: James 1:25 *If you keep looking steadily into God's perfect law— the law that sets you free—and if you do what it says and don't forget what you heard, then God will bless you for doing it.*

BIBLE

How can a book written so long ago be relevant for me today?

H e b r e w s   4 : 1 2 *The word of God is full of living power. It is sharper than the sharpest knife, cutting deep into our innermost thoughts and desires. It exposes us for what we really are.*

The word of God is as contemporary as the heart of God and as relevant as our most urgent need a heartbeat ago.

Why is it important to memorize Scripture?

D e u t e r o n o m y   3 0 : 1 4 *The message is very close at hand; it is on your lips and in your heart so that you can obey it.*

P s a l m   3 7 : 3 1 *They fill their hearts with God's law, so they will never slip from his path.*

P s a l m   1 1 9 : 1 1 *I have hidden your word in my heart, that I might not sin against you.*

What you fill your heart and mind with is what you become. Memorizing Scripture helps you meditate on God's life-changing words at any time.

Can the Bible give me guidance?

P s a l m   1 1 9 : 1 0 5 *Your word is a lamp for my feet and a light for my path.*

Proverbs 6:23 *These commands and this teaching are a lamp to light the way ahead of you.* The word of God is from the mind and heart of God, and who can deny that the all-wise, all-powerful, ever-present God is the best guide of all?

Can the Bible give me comfort?

Psalm 119:49-50 *Remember your promise to me, for it is my only hope. . . . It comforts me in all my troubles.*

Romans 15:4 *The Scriptures . . . give us hope and encouragement as we wait patiently for God's promises.*
The Bible is filled with God's promises that give us comfort and encouragement in this life as well as the confident assurance that we will one day live forever in peace and security with him.

PROMISE FROM GOD: Psalm 119:89 *Forever, O LORD, your word stands firm in heaven.*

BLAME

What can I do to live a blameless life?

1 Corinthians 1:8 *He will keep you strong right up to the end, and he will keep you free from all blame on the great day when our Lord Jesus Christ returns.*

Christ is the one who gives us strength and makes us blameless.

Colossians 1:22 *Now he has brought you back as his friends. He has done this through his death on the cross in his own human body. As a result, he has brought you into the very presence of God, and you are holy and blameless as you stand before him without a single fault.*

There is no way that we alone could ever live a blameless life. It is only through Christ dying on the cross that we are found blameless.

Since it is impossible for me to live blamelessly, does it really matter if I go out and sin occasionally?

Philippians 2:14-15 *In everything you do, stay away from complaining and arguing, so that no one can speak a word of blame against you. You are to live clean, innocent lives as children of God in a dark world full of crooked and perverse people. Let your lives shine brightly before them.*

29

Our responsibility is to live as Christ's examples. To do this, we must keep our hearts and minds pure.

PROMISE FROM GOD:
2 Corinthians 13:11 *Rejoice. Change your ways. Encourage each other. . . . Then the God of love and peace will be with you.*

BROKENNESS

Why is brokenness an important attitude for us to develop?

Psalm 51:17 *The sacrifice you want is a broken spirit. A broken and repentant heart, O God, you will not despise.*
God wants us to be brokenhearted about our sin.

Psalm 147:3 *He heals the brokenhearted, binding up their wounds.*
When we turn to God in brokenness over our sin, he begins to heal us and restore us.

Job 2:8-10 *Job scraped his skin with a piece of broken pottery as he sat among the ashes. His wife said to him, "Are you still trying to maintain your integrity? Curse God and die."*
The alternative to brokenness before God is bitterness, which leads to death.

Isaiah 66:2 *I will bless those who have humble and contrite hearts, who tremble at my word.*
Even when there is no sin to require a broken attitude, God will bless us when we maintain our brokenness—our deep humility and dependence on him.

How do we achieve an attitude of brokenness?

Job 42:5-6 *I had heard about you before, but now I have seen you with my own eyes. I take back everything I said, and I sit in dust and ashes to show my repentance.*
Brokenness comes in response to the realization of God's holiness and our own sinfulness.

How should we respond when our hearts are broken?

Psalm 61:1-2 *O God, listen to my cry! Hear my prayer! From the ends of the earth, I will cry to you for help, for my heart is overwhelmed. Lead me to the towering rock of safety.*

Lamentations 1:20 *"LORD, see my anguish! My heart is broken and my soul despairs, for I have rebelled against you. In the streets the sword kills, and at home there is only death."*
When we experience deep grief, it is always right for us to fall before God with an attitude of brokenness.

PROMISE FROM GOD: Psalm
34:18 *The LORD is close to the brokenhearted; he
rescues those who are crushed in spirit.*

BURNOUT

How do I know if I am experiencing burnout?

2 Samuel 21:15 *When David and his men
were in the thick of battle, David became weak and
exhausted.*

Psalm 38:8 *I am exhausted and completely
crushed. My groans come from an anguished heart.*
If we become weak and exhausted in the middle
of doing our work, we may be experiencing
burnout.

1 Kings 19:14 *I alone am left, and now they are
trying to kill me, too.*
We may be experiencing burnout if we despair
because our work seems fruitless.

Psalm 69:1-2 *The floodwaters are up to my neck.
Deeper and deeper I sink into the mire; I can't find a
foothold to stand on.*
It may be burnout if we feel overwhelmed by
everything that is going on in our lives.

Jeremiah 45:3 *You have said, "I am overwhelmed with trouble! Haven't I had enough pain already? And now the LORD has added more!"*
When we become burned out, we may feel bitter toward God.

What is the antidote for burnout?

Exodus 18:21-23 *Find some capable, honest men. . . . They will help you carry the load, making the task easier for you. If you follow this advice, . . . then you will be able to endure the pressures.*
Sometimes we might be able to delegate some of our workload.

Exodus 23:12 *"Work for six days, and rest on the seventh. . . . It will . . . allow the people of your household . . . to be refreshed."*
Regular, consistent, weekly rest is an important part of avoiding and recovering from burnout.

2 Samuel 17:28-29 *They brought sleeping mats, cooking pots, serving bowls, wheat and barley flour, roasted grain, beans, lentils, honey, butter, sheep, and cheese for David and those who were with him. For they said, "You must all be very tired and hungry and thirsty after your long march through the wilderness."*

1 Kings 19:5-8 *As he was sleeping, an angel touched him and told him, "Get up and eat!" . . . So he ate and drank and lay down again. Then the angel of the LORD came again and touched him and said, "Get up and eat some more, for there is a long journey ahead of you." So he got up and ate and drank.*
Getting solid meals and good sleep will help us overcome burnout.

Nehemiah 6:9 *So I prayed for strength to continue the work.*

2 Thessalonians 2:16-17 *May our Lord Jesus Christ and God our Father . . . comfort your hearts and give you strength in every good thing you do and say.*
Sometimes we can't stop working, even though we feel exhausted, but we can encourage each other and pray to God for strength to keep going until we reach a stopping place.

Isaiah 30:15 *Only in returning to me and waiting for me will you be saved. In quietness and confidence is your strength.*

Matthew 11:28-29 *Come to me, all of you who are weary and carry heavy burdens, and I will give you rest . . . and you will find rest for your souls.*
We should renew our fellowship with God and be restored by spending time with him.

PROMISE FROM GOD: Isaiah 40:29-31 *He gives power to those who are tired and worn out; he offers strength to the weak. Even youths will become exhausted, and young men will give up. But those who wait on the LORD will find new strength. They will fly high on wings like eagles. They will run and not grow weary. They will walk and not faint.*

BUSINESS

Can I be a Christian *and* successful in business?

Proverbs 31:16 *She goes out to inspect a field and buys it; with her earnings she plants a vineyard.*
God thinks highly of people who are enterprising and hardworking.

Acts 18:1-3 *A Jew named Aquila . . . had recently arrived from Italy with his wife, Priscilla. . . . Paul lived and worked with them, for they were tentmakers just as he was.*
Aquila and Priscilla are an example of early Christians who used their successful business to serve God.

Ephesians 6:6-7 *Work hard. . . . As slaves of Christ, do the will of God with all your heart. Work with enthusiasm, as though you were working for the Lord rather than for people.*

When God's people work hard in business, we *are* serving the Lord if we dedicate that work to him.

What principles should guide how I conduct my business?

Ecclesiastes 9:10 *Whatever you do, do well.*

If God has called us to do business, then we should do it well!

Genesis 23:7-16 *Abraham bowed low before them and said, ". . . Let me have the cave of Machpelah. . . . I want to pay the full price, of course." . . . "No, sir," he said to Abraham, "please listen to me. I will give you the cave and the field." . . . Abraham bowed again to the people of the land. . . . "No, listen to me," he insisted. "I will buy it from you. Let me pay the full price for the field." . . . "Well," Ephron answered, "the land is worth four hundred pieces of silver, but what is that between friends?" . . . So Abraham paid Ephron the amount he had suggested, four hundred pieces of silver, as was publicly agreed.*

Abraham's interaction with Ephron is a model of the kind of respect that we should show toward others when we do business with them.

Deuteronomy 25:15-16 *Yes, use honest weights and measures, so that you will enjoy a long life in the land the LORD your God is giving you. Those who cheat with dishonest weights and measures are detestable to the LORD your God.*

Ezekiel 22:12 *There are hired murderers, loan racketeers, and extortioners everywhere! They never even think of me and my commands, says the Sovereign LORD.*

God condemns dishonest and violent means to become successful.

Ruth 4:1-9 *So Boaz went to the town gate and took a seat there. . . . "Come over here, friend. I want to talk to you." . . . Then Boaz called ten leaders from the town and asked them to sit as witnesses. . . . "You are witnesses that today I have bought from Naomi all the property of Elimelech, Kilion, and Mahlon."*

Like Boaz, we should always conduct our business above board and "in public," with no hidden kickbacks or shady deals.

Psalm 112:5 *All goes well for those who are generous, who lend freely and conduct their business fairly.*

It is important for us to be generous in our business dealings—it is an investment that will certainly come back to us later!

Amos 8:4-5 *Listen to this, you who rob the poor and trample the needy! You can't wait for the Sabbath day to be over and the religious festivals to end so you can get back to cheating the helpless.* Serving God through our business means that we live in harmony with what we profess on Sundays.

Mark 12:17 *"Well, then," Jesus said, "give to Caesar what belongs to him. But everything that belongs to God must be given to God."* We must always be sure that we pay all of our taxes that are due.

Luke 14:28 *Don't begin until you count the cost.* Whenever we start a project or a business venture, we had better plan ahead and make sure that we can carry it through.

James 4:13-15 *Look here, you people who say, "Today or tomorrow we are going to a certain town and will stay there a year. We will do business there and make a profit." How do you know what will happen tomorrow? For your life is like the morning fog—it's here a little while, then it's gone. What you ought to say is, "If the Lord wants us to, we will live and do this or that."* Whatever business ventures we pursue, we must always remember that God is our Lord and that we are completely dependent on him in everything.

PROMISE FROM GOD: Psalm
37:37 *Look at those who are honest and good, for a*
wonderful future lies before those who love peace.

CALL OF GOD

Has God called me to do specific things?

Ecclesiastes 11:9 *Do everything you want to*
do; take it all in. But remember that you must give an
account to God for everything you do.
God gives us the freedom to do what we think is
best, but we will answer for everything we do.

Jeremiah 1:4-5 *The LORD gave me a message. . . .*
"I knew you before I formed you in your mother's
womb. Before you were born I set you apart and
appointed you as my spokesman to the world."
Sometimes God may call us to fulfill a very
specific ministry. When that happens, he will
make sure that we know it.

1 Corinthians 12:4-7 *There are different*
kinds of spiritual gifts, but it is the same Holy Spirit
who is the source of them all. . . . A spiritual gift is
given to each of us as a means of helping the entire
church.

2 Timothy 4:5 *Complete the ministry God has given you.*
God has given each of us a special ministry that he wants us to perform in the church to build up the body and bring glory to his name.

How do I know what my calling is?

Psalm 119:105 *Your word is a lamp for my feet and a light for my path.*
The first step in knowing our calling is to get to know God intimately through his word and let him guide us through it in everything.

Daniel 1:17 *God gave these four young men an unusual aptitude for learning the literature and science of the time.*
God has given each of us special aptitudes and abilities. These help us to see the kinds of things that we should be doing.

Acts 20:24 *My life is worth nothing unless I use it for doing the work assigned me by the Lord Jesus.*
When God gives us a specific calling, it fills our thoughts and energies, so that we pursue it wholeheartedly.

Romans 12:2 *Let God transform you into a new person by changing the way you think. Then you will know what God wants you to do.*
When we let God transform us by the power of his Holy Spirit, he will show us what he wants us to do.

PROMISE FROM GOD:
1 Thessalonians 5:23-24 *May the God of peace make you holy in every way, and may your whole spirit and soul and body be kept blameless until that day when our Lord Jesus Christ comes again. God, who calls you, is faithful; he will do this.*

CHARACTER

What are the attributes of godly character?

Ezekiel 18:5-9 *Suppose a certain man is just and does what is lawful and right, and he has not feasted in the mountains before Israel's idols or worshiped them. And suppose he does not commit adultery. . . . Suppose he is a merciful creditor . . . and does not rob the poor but instead gives food to the hungry and provides clothes for people in need. And suppose he grants loans without interest, stays away from injustice, is honest and fair when judging others, and faithfully obeys my laws and regulations. Anyone who does these things is just and will surely live, says the Sovereign LORD.* Justice, righteousness, mercy, honesty, fairness, and faithfulness are essential traits of godly character.

How can I develop greater character?

Deuteronomy 8:2 Remember how the LORD your God led you through the wilderness for forty years, humbling you and testing you to prove your character, and to find out whether or not you would really obey his commands.

You are not born with godly character; it is developed through experience and testing and a commitment to knowing God and his word.

PROMISE FROM GOD: *James 1:4 When your endurance is fully developed, you will be strong in character and ready for anything.*

CHEATING

What does God think of cheating? Is it always wrong?

Proverbs 11:1 The LORD hates cheating, but he delights in honesty.

Cheating violates God's holiness.

Is some cheating worse than other cheating?

Mark 12:40 *They shamelessly cheat widows out of their property, and then, to cover up the kind of people they really are, they make long prayers in public. Because of this, their punishment will be the greater.*

Covering cheating with a pious sugar coating is doubly wrong: first the cheating, and second the pious deceit. God hates both.

Can we cheat ourselves?

Luke 16:10 *Unless you are faithful in small matters, you won't be faithful in large ones. If you cheat even a little, you won't be honest with greater responsibilities.*

When we cheat, we are actually cheating ourselves of what God has planned for us.

How do we cheat God?

Malachi 3:8 *Should people cheat God? Yet you have cheated me! But you ask, "What do you mean? When did we ever cheat you?" You have cheated me of the tithes and offerings due to me.*

We cheat God when we do not give to him what he deserves.

PROMISE FROM GOD: Romans
13:9-10 *The commandments against adultery and
murder and stealing and coveting—and any other
commandment—are all summed up in this one
commandment: "Love your neighbor as yourself."
Love does no wrong to anyone, so love satisfies all of
God's requirements.*

CHOICES

What are some principles for making good choices?

Deuteronomy 30:19-20 *Oh, that you would
choose life, that you and your descendants might live!
Choose to love the LORD your God and to obey him
and commit yourself to him, for he is your life.*
We should always make choices that bring life.

Psalm 119:11 *I have hidden your word in my
heart, that I might not sin against you.*
Listening continually to God's voice in his word
will help us to see what is right and what is
wrong.

Proverbs 11:14 *With many counselors, there is
safety.*
Another good way to ensure good choices is to
weigh carefully the advice of reliable counselors.

Hebrews 11:8, 25-27 *It was by faith that Abraham obeyed when God called him to leave home. . . . It was by faith that Moses . . . chose to share the oppression of God's people instead of enjoying the fleeting pleasures of sin. . . . It was by faith that Moses left the land of Egypt. . . . Moses kept right on going because he kept his eyes on the one who is invisible.*

When we let faith in God guide our actions, we are much more likely to make good choices.

PROMISE FROM GOD: Psalm 73:24 *You will keep on guiding me with your counsel, leading me to a glorious destiny.*

CHRISTLIKENESS

What is meant by Christlikeness?

Luke 9:23 *He said to the crowd, "If any of you wants to be my follower, you must put aside your selfish ambition, shoulder your cross daily, and follow me."*

Christlikeness involves selflessly following Christ.

Luke 6:36 *You must be compassionate, just as your Father is compassionate.*

A compassionate lifestyle is a sign of Christlikeness.

1 Peter 2:21-23 *Christ, who suffered for you, is your example. Follow in his steps. . . . He did not retaliate when he was insulted. When he suffered, he did not threaten to get even. He left his case in the hands of God, who always judges fairly.*
Christlikeness is following in Christ's footsteps. As we follow our Lord, we attract others to follow him also.

John 13:14-15 *Since I, the Lord and Teacher, have washed your feet, you ought to wash each other's feet. I have given you an example to follow. Do as I have done to you.*
A life of humble service is a necessary part of Christlikeness.

How can I show Christlikeness to my enemies?

Luke 6:32-33 *Do you think you deserve credit merely for loving those who love you? Even the sinners do that! And if you do good only to those who do good to you, is that so wonderful? Even sinners do that much!*
We show them Christ by treating them with Christ's love.

Matthew 5:44 *But I say, love your enemies! Pray for those who persecute you!*

Galatians 5:22-23 *When the Holy Spirit controls our lives, he will produce this kind of fruit in us: love, joy, peace, patience, kindness, goodness, faithfulness, gentleness, and self-control. Here there is no conflict with the law.*

When Christ lives in us and through us, we can show Christlikeness to others. Actually, we can't do it—Christ does.

PROMISE FROM GOD: Galatians 2:20 *I myself no longer live, but Christ lives in me. So I live my life in this earthly body by trusting in the Son of God, who loved me and gave himself for me.*

CHURCH

Why should I be involved in church?

Ephesians 2:19-21 *You are citizens along with all of God's holy people. You are members of God's family. We are his house, built on the foundation of the apostles and the prophets. And the cornerstone is Christ Jesus himself. We who believe are carefully joined together, becoming a holy temple for the Lord.* All believers are joined together to form God's family, which is God's house and God's temple. But only by meeting together can we experience this reality.

Hebrews 10:25 *Let us not neglect our meeting together, as some people do, but encourage and warn each other, especially now that the day of his coming back again is drawing near.*

When we meet together, we can build each other up and help each other. But we can't receive this kind of fellowship if we don't meet with other believers!

What kinds of things should the church do?

Matthew 28:18-20 *Jesus came and told his disciples, "I have been given complete authority in heaven and on earth. Therefore, go and make disciples of all the nations, baptizing them in the name of the Father and the Son and the Holy Spirit. Teach these new disciples to obey all the commands I have given you."*

One of the primary jobs of the church is to make disciples and to teach people God's truth.

Acts 2:42-44 *They joined with the other believers and devoted themselves to the apostles' teaching and fellowship, sharing in the Lord's Supper and in prayer. . . . And all the believers met together constantly and shared everything they had.*

The key functions of the church include teaching, fellowship, worship, and prayer.

Acts 13:2-3 *One day . . . the Holy Spirit said, "Dedicate Barnabas and Saul for the special work I have for them." So after more fasting and prayer, the men laid their hands on them and sent them on their way.*

The church is responsible to send missionaries out who will make God's truth known.

1 Timothy 5:3 *The church should care for any widow who has no one else to care for her.*

God wants the church to take care of those who are poor and needy.

2 Timothy 4:2 *Preach the word of God. Be persistent, whether the time is favorable or not. Patiently correct, rebuke, and encourage your people with good teaching.*

There is a special place in the church for teaching and preaching—the public proclamation of God's word.

James 5:14-15 *Are any among you sick? They should call for the elders of the church and have them pray over them, anointing them with oil in the name of the Lord. And their prayer offered in faith will heal the sick, and the Lord will make them well. And anyone who has committed sins will be forgiven.*

The church should pray for its members who are sick or have other needs.

PROMISE FROM GOD: Matthew 16:18 *Upon this rock I will build my church, and all the powers of hell will not conquer it.*

COMMITMENT

How strong is God's commitment to me?

Isaiah 46:4 *I will be your God throughout your lifetime—until your hair is white with age. I made you, and I will care for you. I will carry you along and save you.*

God has promised his total commitment to us, from the time we are born to the time we die. Nothing can break his commitment.

Titus 2:14 *He gave his life to free us from every kind of sin, to cleanse us, and to make us his very own people, totally committed to doing what is right.*

God's commitment to us is so strong that Jesus gave his life for us.

What is involved in being committed to God?

Exodus 24:3 *The people . . . answered in unison, "We will do everything the LORD has told us to do."*

John 17:1, 4 *Jesus . . . looked up to heaven and said, "Father, . . . I brought glory to you here on earth by doing everything you told me to do."*

God wants us to commit ourselves to doing everything he has told us to do.

Joshua 24:14 *So honor the LORD and serve him wholeheartedly. Put away forever the idols your ancestors worshiped. . . . Serve the LORD alone.*

Matthew 6:24 *No one can serve two masters. For you will hate one and love the other, or be devoted to one and despise the other.*
Wholehearted commitment to God means that we give up other masters, whatever or whomever they may be.

1 Chronicles 29:5 *"Who will follow my example? Who is willing to give offerings to the LORD today?"*

Proverbs 3:9 *Honor the LORD with your wealth and with the best part of everything your land produces.*
If we are truly committed to God, we will gladly give from our material assets.

Amos 5:24 *I want to see a mighty flood of justice, a river of righteous living that will never run dry.*
Commitment to God means commitment to do good to other people.

Romans 6:13 *Give yourselves completely to God since you have been given new life. And use your whole body as a tool to do what is right for the glory of God.*

Wholehearted commitment involves giving him everything, even our bodies, to use as he wishes.

PROMISE FROM GOD:
2 Chronicles 15:15 *Eagerly they sought after God, and they found him.*

COMPASSION

How does God show his compassion to me?

Psalm 103:8 *The LORD is merciful and gracious; he is slow to get angry and full of unfailing love.*
God shows his compassion to us by giving us blessings we don't deserve and by not giving us what we do deserve.

How can I follow Christ's example of compassion to people I associate with daily?

2 Corinthians 8:9 *You know how full of love and kindness our Lord Jesus Christ was. Though he was very rich, yet for your sakes he became poor, so that by his poverty he could make you rich.*
Christ in his love for us gave up his most high position to come to earth and die for us. Our response should be to abandon our pride and show compassion to those around us, even when it takes us out of our comfort zone.

PROMISE FROM GOD: Psalm
1 4 5 : 9 *The LORD is good to everyone. He showers
compassion on all his creation.*

COMPETITION

Can competition be good?
1 Corinthians 9:24 *Remember that in a race
everyone runs, but only one person gets the prize. You
also must run in such a way that you will win.*
Competition can drive us to improve ourselves or
sharpen our skills.

When does competition become a bad thing?
2 Timothy 2:5 *Follow the Lord's rules for doing
his work, just as an athlete either follows the rules or
is disqualified and wins no prize.*
Competitiveness can lead to sin if we try to win
at all costs.

Luke 18:11 *The proud Pharisee stood by himself
and prayed this prayer: "I thank you, God, that I am
not a sinner like everyone else, especially like that tax
collector over there! For I never cheat, I don't sin, I
don't commit adultery."*
Competition can lead to us to compare ourselves
favorably with others. This is pride, and pride
always leads us to trouble.

Are there areas where competition is not appropriate?

Matthew 18:1-4 *About that time the disciples came to Jesus and asked, "Which of us is greatest in the Kingdom of Heaven?". . . . Then [Jesus] said, ". . . Anyone who becomes as humble as this little child is the greatest in the Kingdom of Heaven."*
Competition is inappropriate any time we elevate ourselves over others.

People say I can be too competitive at times. How can I learn to lighten up?

Matthew 6:19-20 *Don't store up treasures here on earth. . . . Store your treasures in heaven.*
We are warned not to spend our lives competing for the wrong things for the wrong reasons.

Colossians 3:23 *Work hard and cheerfully at whatever you do, as though you were working for the Lord rather than for people.*
We are called to work hard to do our best, not to beat others. Our best honors the God who created us.

PROMISE FROM GOD:
1 Corinthians 15:57 *How we thank God, who gives us victory over sin and death through Jesus Christ our Lord!*

54

COMPLAINING

What are the dangers of complaining?

James 4:11 *Don't speak evil against each other, my dear brothers and sisters. If you criticize each other and condemn each other, then you are criticizing and condemning God's law. But you are not a judge who can decide whether the law is right or wrong. Your job is to obey it.*

James 5:9 *Don't grumble about each other, my brothers and sisters, or God will judge you. For look! The great Judge is coming. He is standing at the door!* Complaining about others is really complaining about God and his word.

How should I react to others' complaints about me?

Proverbs 15:31-32 *If you listen to constructive criticism, you will be at home among the wise. If you reject criticism, you only harm yourself; but if you listen to correction, you grow in understanding.* Constructive criticism should always be welcomed if it is given in a spirit of love.

What should we do instead of complaining?

Philippians 2:14-15 *In everything you do, stay away from complaining and arguing. . . . You are to live clean, innocent lives as children of God. . . . Let your lives shine brightly before them.*

Instead of complaining about others, we should be role models to them.

Lamentations 3:39-40 *Why should we, mere humans, complain when we are punished for our sins? Instead, let us test and examine our ways. Let us turn again in repentance to the LORD.*
Instead of complaining about the sins of others, let's repent of our own sins.

Luke 6:37 *Stop judging others, and you will not be judged. Stop criticizing others, or it will all come back on you. If you forgive others, you will be forgiven.*
Instead of complaining about the weaknesses of others, we should forgive them as we would like to be forgiven.

PROMISE FROM GOD: Ephesians 4:29 *Let everything you say be good and helpful, so that your words will be an encouragement to those who hear them.*

COMPROMISE

What is the difference between compromising and negotiating?

Daniel 1:8 *Daniel made up his mind not to defile himself by eating the food and wine given to them by the king. He asked the chief official for permission to eat other things instead.*

Compromising and negotiating both have the same end goal—the greater good for all parties involved. Daniel was able to negotiate a settlement without compromising his convictions—both the king and Daniel got what they wanted. Whenever you negotiate, never give up your Christian convictions.

When is compromise inappropriate?

Romans 6:12 *Do not let sin control the way you live; do not give in to its lustful desires.*
Compromise is inappropriate when it involves sin of any kind.

1 Samuel 15:24 *Saul finally admitted, "Yes, I have sinned. I have disobeyed your instructions and the LORD's command, for I was afraid of the people and did what they demanded."*

3 John 1:11 *Dear friend, don't let this bad example influence you. Follow only what is good.*
When compromise is motivated by people pleasing or following the bad example of others, it is inappropriate.

When is compromise appropriate?

Romans 14:15 *If another Christian is distressed by what you eat, you are not acting in love if you eat it. Don't let your eating ruin someone for whom Christ died.*

Maintaining unity in the body of Christ may require compromising personal preferences.

Romans 15:1 *We may know that these things make no difference, but we cannot just go ahead and do them to please ourselves. We must be considerate of the doubts and fears of those who think these things are wrong.*
We must be willing to compromise what pleases us for the sake of others' doubts and fears.

Philippians 2:2 *Make me truly happy by agreeing wholeheartedly with each other, loving one another, and working together with one heart and purpose.*
Agreement may mean giving up something *I* want for the sake of what *we* want.

PROMISE FROM GOD:
1 Chronicles 22:13 *If you carefully obey the laws and regulations that the LORD gave to Israel through Moses, you will be successful. Be strong and courageous; do not be afraid or lose heart!*

CONFESSION

What is involved in true confession?
2 Chronicles 7:14 *If my people who are called by my name will humble themselves and pray and seek my face and turn from their wicked ways, I will hear from heaven and will forgive their sins and heal their land.*

Psalm 51:3-4, 6, 17 *I recognize my shameful deeds—they haunt me day and night. Against you, and you alone, have I sinned; I have done what is evil in your sight. . . . But you desire honesty from the heart, so you can teach me to be wise in my inmost being. . . . The sacrifice you want is a broken spirit. A broken and repentant heart, O God, you will not despise.*

Psalm 38:18 *I confess my sins; I am deeply sorry for what I have done.*

Proverbs 28:13 *People who cover over their sins will not prosper. But if they confess and forsake them, they will receive mercy.*
Sorrow for our sin, humility before God, seeking God and his forgiveness, turning to God in prayer, turning from sin—these are ingredients of confession to God.

To whom should we direct our confession?

Ezra 10:11 *Confess your sin to the LORD, the God of your ancestors, and do what he demands.*

1 Chronicles 21:8 *David said to God, "I have sinned greatly and shouldn't have taken the census. Please forgive me for doing this foolish thing."*

Psalm 41:4 *"O LORD," I prayed, "have mercy on me. Heal me, for I have sinned against you."*
Confess sin to God, because all sin is against him.

When is it appropriate to confess our sins to others?

Numbers 5:6-7 *If any of the people—men or women—betray the LORD by doing wrong to another person, they are guilty. They must confess their sin and make full restitution for what they have done, adding a penalty of 20 percent and returning it to the person who was wronged.*

James 5:16 *Confess your sins to each other and pray for each other so that you may be healed.*
We should confess our sins to others when we have wronged them and need their forgiveness.

Does God's forgiveness always follow true confession?

Psalm 86:5 *O Lord, you are so good, so ready to forgive, so full of unfailing love for all who ask your aid.*
God's supply of forgiveness far exceeds the number of times we could ever go to him for forgiveness.

PROMISE FROM GOD: 1 John 1:9
If we confess our sins to him, he is faithful and just to forgive us and to cleanse us from every wrong.

CONFLICT

How does conflict arise?

Proverbs 13:10 *Pride leads to arguments.*

Proverbs 28:25 *Greed causes fighting.*

Proverbs 30:33 *Anger causes quarrels.*
Pride, greed, anger—these are all aspects of our sinful, human nature, and these are the things that bring us into conflict with other people.

Romans 7:22-23 *I love God's law with all my heart. But there is another law at work within me that is at war with my mind. This law wins the fight and makes me a slave to the sin that is still within me.*
Those who follow Christ also experience conflict within themselves between the old sinful nature and the new spiritual nature.

What is the right way to handle conflict or disagreement?

1 Corinthians 6:7 *To have such lawsuits at all is a real defeat for you. Why not just accept the injustice and leave it at that? Why not let yourselves be cheated?*
We might have to give up our rights in order to resolve a conflict of interests.

John 17:21 *"My prayer for all of them is that they will be one, just as you and I are one, Father."*

61

We should pray for peace and unity with other people.

Acts 15:36-39 *Barnabas . . . wanted to take along John Mark. But Paul disagreed strongly . . . Their disagreement over this was so sharp that they separated.*
Sometimes differences of opinion are so strong that no resolution seems possible and a parting of ways is necessary.

2 Timothy 2:24-25 *The Lord's servants must not quarrel but must be kind to everyone. They must . . . be patient with difficult people. They should gently teach those who oppose the truth.*
When people disagree with what we are saying, we should maintain a gracious and gentle attitude instead of becoming angry and defensive.

PROMISE FROM GOD: Matthew 5:9 *God blesses those who work for peace, for they will be called the children of God.*

CONFRONTATION

Under what circumstances should we confront?

Ephesians 5:11 *Take no part in the worthless deeds of evil and darkness; instead, rebuke and expose them.*

Evil and wickedness must be confronted, or else it may consume us.

2 Samuel 12:1, 7 *So the LORD sent Nathan the prophet to tell David this story. . . . Then Nathan said to David, "You are that man!"*
Confronting someone who does wrong may lead them back into reconciliation with God and others.

How do we effectively confront others?
Nehemiah 13:11 *I immediately confronted the leaders and demanded, "Why has the Temple of God been neglected?" Then I called all the Levites back again and restored them to their proper duties.*
When it is necessary, confrontation is best done as soon as possible.

Titus 3:2 *They must not speak evil of anyone, and they must avoid quarreling. Instead, they should be gentle and show true humility to everyone.*
It is essential to consider how we would want someone to speak to us about a problem in our life.

2 Timothy 1:7 *God has not given us a spirit of fear and timidity, but of power, love, and self-discipline.*
If confrontation is necessary, ask God to give you the power, love, and self-discipline to say what you must.

How should we respond when others confront us?

Proverbs 24:26 *It is an honor to receive an honest reply.*
We should be honored that someone cares enough about us to want what is best for us.

PROMISE FROM GOD: Proverbs 19:25 *If you punish a mocker, the simpleminded will learn a lesson; if you reprove the wise, they will be all the wiser.*

CONSEQUENCES

What are the consequences of sin?

Romans 5:12 *Adam's sin brought death.*

Ezekiel 3:20 *If good people turn bad and don't listen to my warning, they will die.*
Sin brings separation from God and spiritual death.

Genesis 3:17 *To Adam he said, "Because you . . . ate the fruit I told you not to eat, I have placed a curse on the ground. All your life you will struggle to scratch a living from it."*
Hardship and difficulty are consequences of sin.

Jeremiah 11:8 *Your ancestors did not pay any attention; they would not even listen. Instead, they stubbornly followed their own evil desires. And because they refused to obey, I brought upon them all the curses described in our covenant.*
Sin invites God's curse upon us.

Psalm 7:14-16 *The wicked . . . dig a pit to trap others and then fall into it themselves. They make trouble, but it backfires on them. They plan violence for others, but it falls on their own heads.*
The evil we plan for others may come back to destroy us.

Proverbs 18:21 *Those who love to talk will experience the consequences, for the tongue can kill or nourish life.*
Evil words may return to condemn us.

Do we ever suffer the consequences of another person's sin?

Romans 5:12 *Adam's sin brought death, so death spread to everyone, for everyone sinned.*
We do suffer the consequences of Adam's sin, but it is also our own sin. We, too, have sinned and deserve death.

Isaiah 10:1-2 *Destruction is certain for the unjust judges, for those who issue unfair laws. They deprive the poor, the widows, and the orphans of justice. Yes, they rob widows and fatherless children!* The poor, the widows, and the orphans sometimes have to live with the reality of others' sins, but God will make certain that justice is served.

Ezekiel 18:20 *The one who sins is the one who dies.*
We each reap the consequences of our own actions.

PROMISE FROM GOD: Hosea 10:12 *Plant the good seeds of righteousness, and you will harvest a crop of my love. Plow up the hard ground of your hearts, for now is the time to seek the LORD, that he may come and shower righteousness upon you.*

CONTENTMENT

How can I find contentment regardless of life's circumstances?

2 Corinthians 12:10 *Since I know it is all for Christ's good, I am quite content with my weaknesses and with insults, hardships, persecutions, and calamities.*

Philippians 4:11-13 *I have learned how to get along happily whether I have much or little. I know how to live on almost nothing or with everything. I have learned the secret of living in every situation, whether it is with a full stomach or empty, with plenty or little. For I can do everything with the help of Christ who gives me the strength I need.*

When we depend on circumstances for our contentment, we become unhappy when things don't go our way. When we depend on Jesus for our contentment, we are secure because he never fails.

In what or whom should I find contentment?

Psalm 107:8-9 *Let them praise the LORD for his great love and for all his wonderful deeds to them. For he satisfies the thirsty and fills the hungry with good things.*

Psalm 119:35 *Make me walk along the path of your commands, for that is where my happiness is found.*

Psalm 90:14 *Satisfy us in the morning with your unfailing love, so we may sing for joy to the end of our lives.*

God, who is the source of every good thing, can certainly satisfy our needs and give us contentment.

What is the relationship between wealth and contentment?

1 Timothy 6:17 *Tell those who are rich in this world not to be proud and not to trust in their money, which will soon be gone. But their trust should be in the living God, who richly gives us all we need for our enjoyment.*

Ecclesiastes 5:10 *Those who love money will never have enough. How absurd to think that wealth brings true happiness!*
Money and possessions can easily deceive us into thinking, *If only I had a little more, I would be content.* Nothing could be farther from the truth.

Hebrews 13:5 *Stay away from the love of money; be satisfied with what you have. For God has said, "I will never fail you. I will never forsake you."*

1 Timothy 6:6-7 *True religion with contentment is great wealth. After all, we didn't bring anything with us when we came into the world, and we certainly cannot carry anything with us when we die.*
Contentment is not related to how much material wealth we have but to how much of God's presence is in our lives.

PROMISE FROM GOD: 2 Peter 1:3 *As we know Jesus better, his divine power gives us everything we need for living a godly life. He has called us to receive his own glory and goodness!*

CRISIS

What are some possible reasons for crisis in my life?

Jonah 1:4, 12 *As the ship was sailing along, suddenly the LORD flung a powerful wind over the sea, causing a violent storm that threatened to send them to the bottom. . . . Jonah said, " . . . I know that this terible storm is all my fault."*

Jonah was in crisis for running away from God, but the sailors were in crisis, too, because of Jonah's sin! You can cause others to be in crisis because of your sin. And your crisis could be the result of someone else's sin.

Proverbs 27:12 *A prudent person foresees the danger ahead and takes precautions. The simpleton goes blindly on and suffers the consequences.*

Sometimes a crisis comes because we were not wise in the decisions we made.

2 Corinthians 4:11 *Yes, we live under constant danger of death because we serve Jesus, so that the life of Jesus will be obvious in our dying bodies.*

Sometimes a crisis comes because we serve Jesus, and serving Jesus can bring persecution.

What are some of the blessings that can come from our times of crisis?

Jonah 1:16 *The sailors were awestruck by the LORD's great power, and they offered him a sacrifice and vowed to serve him.*

Sometimes a crisis helps us see God more clearly.

Philippians 1:12 *I want you to know, dear friends, that everything that has happened to me here has helped to spread the Good News.*

How we react to times of crisis can determine what others think about Christ.

Romans 5:3-4 *We can rejoice, too, when we run into problems and trials, for we know that they are good for us—they help us learn to endure. And endurance develops strength of character in us, and character strengthens our confident expectation of salvation.*

Times of crisis can strengthen our character.

1 Peter 4:13 *These trials will make you partners with Christ in his suffering.*

Times of crisis help us identify with the suffering that Jesus endured for our sake.

How should I respond to crisis?

Jonah 2:1 *Then Jonah prayed to the LORD his God from inside the fish.*

Jonah 2:7 *When I had lost all hope, I turned my thoughts once more to the LORD.*

Psalm 130:1 *From the depths of despair, O LORD, I call for your help.*
When we reach the end of our rope, we must call upon the Lord, for our weaknesses are times for his strength; our crises are his opportunities.

Psalm 28:7 *The LORD is my strength, my shield from every danger. I trust in him with all my heart.*
In crisis we may wonder, *Whom can I trust?* We can always trust the Lord.

PROMISE FROM GOD: Psalm 46:1 *God is our refuge and strength, always ready to help in times of trouble.*

CRITICISM

How should I respond to criticism? How do I evaluate whether it is constructive or destructive?

Proverbs 12:16-17 *A wise person stays calm when insulted. An honest witness tells the truth; a false witness tells lies.*
If you are criticized, stay calm and don't lash back. Evaluate whether the criticism is coming from a person with a reputation for truth or lies. Ask yourself if the criticism is meant to heal or hurt.

1 Corinthians 4:4 *My conscience is clear, but that isn't what matters. It is the Lord himself who will examine me and decide.*

Always work to maintain a clear conscience by being honest and trustworthy. This allows you to shrug off criticism you know is unjustified.

1 Peter 4:14 *Be happy if you are insulted for being a Christian, for then the glorious Spirit of God will come upon you.*

Consider it a privilege to be criticized for your faith in God.

Should we be careful about criticizing others?

Romans 14:10 *Why do you condemn another Christian? . . . Remember, each of us will stand personally before the judgment seat of God.*

James 4:11 *If you criticize each other and condemn each other, then you are criticizing and condemning God's law.*

We have no right to give depreciating criticism of another, for that is trying to be a judge over that person, and God alone is our judge.

How do we prevent unjust criticism against us?

Romans 14:18 *If you serve Christ with this attitude, you will please God. And other people will approve of you, too.*

Matthew 7:1 *Stop judging others, and you will not be judged.*
We will often avoid criticism by avoiding words and actions that warrant criticism.

PROMISE FROM GOD: Romans 14:18 *If you serve Christ with this attitude, you will please God. And other Christians will approve of you, too.*

CROSS

What does the cross represent?

Luke 23:32 *Two others, both criminals, were led out to be executed with him.*

Galatians 3:13 *Cursed is everyone who is hung on a tree.*

Philippians 2:8 *In human form he obediently humbled himself even further by dying a criminal's death on a cross.*
The cross was a Roman instrument of capital punishment, a form of execution reserved for the worst criminals, the most shameful death imaginable.

1 Peter 1:18-19 *You know that God paid a ransom to save you from the empty life you inherited from your ancestors. . . . He paid for you with the precious lifeblood of Christ, the sinless, spotless Lamb of God.*

The cross is a symbol of the price that Christ paid to ransom us from sin and death.

Mark 8:34-35 *If any of you wants to be my follower . . . you must put aside your selfish ambition, shoulder your cross, and follow me. If you try to keep your life for yourself, you will lose it. But if you give up your life for my sake and for the sake of the Good News, you will find true life.*

Christ used the cross as a picture of the kind of commitment that he expects from his followers—a commitment that makes us willing to suffer anything, including torture, ridicule, shame, and death, for the sake of Christ.

1 John 3:16 *We know what real love is because Christ gave up his life for us. And so we also ought to give up our lives for our Christian brothers and sisters.*

Because of the extreme sacrifice involved in Christ's willingness to die on a cross, the cross represents the kind of love that we are called to have for our Christian brothers and sisters.

Revelation 12:11 *They have defeated him because of the blood of the Lamb and because of their testimony. And they were not afraid to die.*
Christ's blood and his cross represent the ultimate victory that we have in him.

Why did Jesus have to die on the cross?

Colossians 2:14 *He canceled the record that contained the charges against us. He took it and destroyed it by nailing it to Christ's cross.*
Christ's death was necessary to take away the guilty verdict against us and the judgment that was waiting for us as a result of our sin.

Romans 6:6 *Our old sinful selves were crucified with Christ so that sin might lose its power in our lives. We are no longer slaves to sin.*

Titus 2:14 *He gave his life to free us from every kind of sin, to cleanse us, and to make us his very own people, totally committed to doing what is right.*
Christ's death on the cross was the only way for us to be saved from the power of sin over our lives.

Colossians 1:20 *By him God reconciled everything to himself. He made peace with everything in heaven and on earth by means of his blood on the cross.*

Christ's death was the means God used to bring us back to himself—to reconcile us with him and to bring us into intimate fellowship with him.

Romans 6:23 *The wages of sin is death, but the free gift of God is eternal life through Christ Jesus our Lord.*
Without Christ's death on the cross, we would face eternal condemnation and death. But by his cross Christ offers us the free gift of eternal life.

PROMISE FROM GOD: Hebrews 9:14 *Just think how much more the blood of Christ will purify our hearts from deeds that lead to death so that we can worship the living God. For by the power of the eternal Spirit, Christ offered himself to God as a perfect sacrifice for our sins.*

DEATH

What happens when someone dies?

1 Thessalonians 4:13 *I want you to know what will happen to the Christians who have died.*

1 Corinthians 15:52 *When the trumpet sounds, the Christians who have died will be raised with transformed bodies.*

Revelation 14:11 *They will have no relief day or night, for they have worshiped the beast and his statue and have accepted the mark of his name.*

Revelation 20:15 *Anyone whose name was not found recorded in the Book of Life was thrown into the lake of fire.*

Revelation 21:3 *Look, the home of God is now among his people!*
A Christian who dies will live with God forever. A person who is not a Christian will be condemned to eternal punishment.

How do I keep a proper perspective about death? Why am I so afraid of it?

Colossians 3:1-2 *Since you have been raised to new life with Christ, set your sights on the realities of heaven. . . . Let heaven fill your thoughts.*

2 Corinthians 5:4 *We want to slip into our new bodies so that these dying bodies will be swallowed up by everlasting life.*
Fear of the unknown is natural, and fear of death can be healthy if it draws us to know more about God. It is helpful to think of death as a beginning, not an end. It is our entrance into eternal life with God.

Philippians 1:21 *To me, living is for Christ, and dying is even better.*
A fear of death may be an indication of a weak relationship with God. You must be ready to die (be at peace with yourself) in order to appreciate life fully.

Romans 8:10 *Since Christ lives within you, even though your body will die because of sin, your spirit is alive because you have been made right with God.*
When we accept Christ, we are given eternal life. This does not prevent the death of our body, but it does assure true life with him in heaven forever. And isn't that the life that counts the most?

In life after death, do we keep these bodies or get new ones, or do we have no bodies at all?

1 Corinthians 15:42 *Our earthly bodies, which die and decay, will be different when they are resurrected, for they will never die.*
Our present bodies get sick and become a burden for us. They age and deteriorate. We wouldn't really want to live in them forever. Think how many problems we would accumulate in a few thousand years! We will welcome the new bodies God gives us when we die and leave these present bodies behind.

PROMISE FROM GOD: John 11:25 *Jesus told her, "I am the resurrection and the life. Those who believe in me, even though they die like everyone else, will live again."*

DEBT

See MONEY

DECEIT

What does God think of lying and other forms of deception?

Psalm 5:6 *You will destroy those who tell lies. The LORD detests murderers and deceivers.*

Proverbs 6:16-19 *There are six things the LORD hates—no, seven things he detests: haughty eyes, a lying tongue, . . . a false witness who pours out lies.*

God hates deception and lying.

Psalm 101:7 *I will not allow deceivers to serve me, and liars will not be allowed to enter my presence.*

Isaiah 59:2-3 *There is a problem—your sins have cut you off from God. . . . Your mouth is full of lies, and your lips are tainted with corruption.*

Deceit creates a barrier between us and God.

Zephaniah 3:13 *The people of Israel who survive will do no wrong to each other, never telling lies or deceiving one another. They will live peaceful lives, lying down to sleep in safety; there will be no one to make them afraid.*

Those who practice honesty and not deception
will be blessed by God.

Is deception *always* wrong?

Leviticus 19:11 *Do not steal. Do not cheat one
another. Do not lie.*

Colossians 3:9 *Don't lie to each other, for you
have stripped off your old evil nature and all its
wicked deeds.*

Proverbs 24:28 *Do not testify spitefully against
innocent neighbors; don't lie about them.*
God has commanded us not to lie, and he has
made clear how much he hates deception.

Joshua 2:4-6 *Rahab, who had hidden the two
men, replied, "The men were here earlier, but I didn't
know where they were from. They left the city at dusk,
as the city gates were about to close, and I don't know
where they went. If you hurry, you can probably catch
up with them." (But she had taken them up to the
roof and hidden them beneath piles of flax.)*

Hebrews 11:31 *It was by faith that Rahab the
prostitute did not die with all the others in her city
who refused to obey God. For she had given a friendly
welcome to the spies.*
It seems that lying is acceptable if—and only
if—it is necessary to protect someone from harm.

1 Peter 2:22 *He never sinned, and he never deceived anyone.*
Christ never lied.

Revelation 21:8 *Cowards who turn away from me, and unbelievers, and the corrupt, . . . and all liars—their doom is in the lake that burns with fire and sulfur. This is the second death.*

Revelation 21:27 *Nothing evil will be allowed to enter—no one who practices shameful idolatry and dishonesty—but only those whose names are written in the Lamb's Book of Life.*
Those who practice deceit face eternal judgment in hell.

PROMISE FROM GOD: Psalm 32:2 *Yes, what joy for those whose record the LORD has cleared of sin, whose lives are lived in complete honesty!*

Proverbs 19:5 *A false witness will not go unpunished, nor will a liar escape.*

DELEGATION

See LEADERSHIP

DENIAL

What does it mean to deny God or Christ?

Romans 1:21, 28 *Yes, they knew God, but they wouldn't worship him as God or even give him thanks. . . . They refused to acknowledge God.*

1 John 2:22-23 *Who is the great liar? The one who says that Jesus is not the Christ. Such people are antichrists, for they have denied the Father and the Son. Anyone who denies the Son doesn't have the Father either.*

Refusing to acknowledge God as God, or Christ as Savior, is to deny him.

Matthew 26:69-70 *"You were one of those with Jesus the Galilean." But Peter denied it in front of everyone. "I don't know what you are talking about,"* he said.

When we are ashamed of God or Christ, we deny him.

Titus 1:16 *Such people claim they know God, but they deny him by the way they live. They are despicable and disobedient, worthless for doing anything good.*

We can deny God by saying that we know him and then living as though we don't.

What are the consequences of denying God or Christ?

Romans 1:28 *When they refused to acknowledge God, he abandoned them to their evil minds and let them do things that should never be done.*
People who deny that God is God end up becoming increasingly evil.

Matthew 10:32-33 *If anyone denies me here on earth, I will deny that person before my Father in heaven.*

2 Timothy 2:12 *If we deny him, he will deny us.*
Denying Christ has the awful consequence of having Christ deny us before the Father in heaven.

What kinds of self-denial does God call us to?

Proverbs 23:1-2 *When dining with a ruler, pay attention to what is put before you. If you are a big eater, put a knife to your throat.*

Galatians 5:24 *Those who belong to Christ Jesus have nailed the passions and desires of their sinful nature to his cross and crucified them there.*
God calls us to exercise restraint and self-discipline in the way we live.

Luke 14:33 *No one can become my disciple without giving up everything for me.*

Philippians 3:8 *Yes, everything else is worthless when compared with the priceless gain of knowing Christ Jesus my Lord. I have discarded everything else, counting it all as garbage, so that I may have Christ.* Christ calls us to give up everything to be his followers.

PROMISE FROM GOD: Luke 18:29-30 *Jesus replied, "And I assure you, everyone who has given up house or wife or brothers or parents or children, for the sake of the Kingdom of God, will be repaid many times over in this life, as well as receiving eternal life in the world to come."*

DESIRES

Is it OK to want something?

1 Kings 3:5 *That night the LORD appeared to Solomon in a dream, and God said, "What do you want? Ask, and I will give it to you!"*

Proverbs 13:12 *Hope deferred makes the heart sick, but when dreams come true, there is life and joy.* God created desire within us as a means of expressing ourselves. Desire is good and healthy if directed toward the proper object of desire: that which is good and right and God-honoring.

Psalm 73:25 *I desire you more than anything on earth.*

Isaiah 26:8 *LORD, we love to obey your laws; our heart's desire is to glorify your name.*

Jeremiah 29:13 *If you look for me in earnest, you will find me when you seek me.*
Our greatest desire should be to seek after God.

Philippians 4:8 *Fix your thoughts on what is true and honorable and right. Think about things that are pure and lovely and admirable.*
Desiring sin is always wrong. Make sure the object of your desire is good, consistent with God's word, and not harmful to others.

How do I resist evil desires?

James 3:13 *Live a life of steady goodness so that only good deeds will pour forth.*
Keep yourself busy.

Matthew 6:13 *Don't let us yield to temptation, but deliver us from the evil one.*
Pray about it.

2 Chronicles 34:33 *So Josiah removed all detestable idols.*
Take away the source of temptation.

Colossians 3:2 *Let heaven fill your thoughts.*
Fill your mind with God.

Proverbs 15:22 *Plans go wrong for lack of advice; many counselors bring success.*
Find a person willing to help you.

Can God help me change the desires within my heart? How?

Romans 7:6 *Now we can really serve God, not in the old way . . . but in the new way, by the Spirit.*
When we commit our life to God, he gives us a new heart and a new nature, along with a new desire to please him.

Ezra 1:5 *God stirred the hearts of the priests and Levites . . . to return to Jerusalem to rebuild the Temple of the LORD.*
God stirs our hearts with right desires. It is up to us to act on them.

PROMISE FROM GOD: Ezekiel 36:26 *I will give you a new heart with new and right desires, and I will put a new spirit in you. I will take out your stony hearts of sin and give you new, obedient hearts.*

DIFFERENCES

How does God want us to deal with our differences?

Deuteronomy 10:19 *You, too, must show love to foreigners, for you yourselves were once foreigners in the land of Egypt.*
God wants us to show his love toward those who are different from us.

Psalm 133:1-3 *How wonderful it is, how pleasant, when brothers live together in harmony! For harmony is as precious as the fragrant anointing oil. . . . Harmony is as refreshing as the dew. . . . And the LORD has pronounced his blessing, even life forevermore.*

In the church, God wants us to live together in unity.

Proverbs 17:14 *Beginning a quarrel is like opening a floodgate, so drop the matter before a dispute breaks out.*

1 Corinthians 1:10 *Dear brothers and sisters, I appeal to you by the authority of the Lord Jesus Christ to stop arguing among yourselves. Let there be real harmony so there won't be divisions in the church. I plead with you to be of one mind, united in thought and purpose.*

Arguing over our differences of opinion often does more harm than good.

Ephesians 2:14 *Christ himself has made peace between us Jews and you Gentiles by making us all one people. He has broken down the wall of hostility that used to separate us.*

Ephesians 4:3 *Always keep yourselves united in the Holy Spirit, and bind yourselves together with peace.*

God puts very different people together in the church, and then he unites us through the Holy Spirit.

Can our differences help us be stronger?

Proverbs 27:17 *As iron sharpens iron, a friend sharpens a friend.*

Romans 12:5 *So it is with Christ's body. We are all parts of his one body, and each of us has different work to do. And since we are all one body in Christ, we belong to each other, and each of us needs all the others.*

People with different gifts and perspectives *can* make one another stronger. All kinds of instruments are needed in an orchestra.

PROMISE FROM GOD:
2 Corinthians 13:11 *Live in harmony and peace. Then the God of love and peace will be with you.*

DISCERNMENT

See WISDOM

DISHONESTY

See HONESTY

DIVORCE

What are some ways to prevent divorce?

Ephesians 5:24-25 *As the church submits to Christ, so you wives must submit to your husbands in everything. And you husbands must love your wives with the same love Christ showed the church.*

1 Thessalonians 5:11 *Encourage each other and build each other up.*

Couples who love each other with the kind of love Christ showed when he died for us and who seek to please one another and build one another up—these are the couples who will likely remain happy together.

How do I deal with the bitterness I feel from divorce?

Hebrews 12:15 *Watch out that no bitter root of unbelief rises up among you, for whenever it springs up, many are corrupted by its poison.*

If you are a victim of divorce, you may have been hurt badly, you may have been treated unjustly, you may have been humiliated. But if you allow your bitterness to fester and grow, it will overshadow all you do and render you useless for effectively serving God. You must let your bitterness go and forgive so that God's Holy Spirit can continue to work in your life and help you start anew.

Will God forgive me if I do get divorced?

Psalm 103:3 *He forgives all my sins.*

1 John 1:9 *If we confess our sins to him, he is faithful and just to forgive us and to cleanse us from every wrong.*

No sin is beyond God's forgiveness, and nothing others do against us can separate us from God's unconditional love. No matter what has happened to you, let God restore you to wholeness.

What does the Bible say about divorce?

Malachi 2:14-16 *You cry out, "Why has the LORD abandoned us?" I'll tell you why! Because the LORD witnessed the vows you and your wife made to each other on your wedding day. . . . But you have been disloyal. . . . Didn't the LORD make you one . . . ? In body and spirit you are his. . . . So guard yourself; remain loyal. . . . "For I hate divorce!" says the LORD.*

God sees divorce as wrong because it is the breaking of a binding covenant.

Matthew 19:3-9 *Some Pharisees came and tried to trap him with this question: "Should a man be allowed to divorce his wife for any reason?"*

The Old Testament had specific rules concerning divorce and provided for limited remarriage in special cases (Deut. 24:1-4), while at the same time making it clear that divorce is not God's intention (Mal. 2:14-16). The New Testament also makes it clear that divorce is wrong (Matt. 5:31-32; 1 Cor. 7:10-11, 15-16), but allows for limited exceptions, as mentioned in these passages.

PROMISE FROM GOD: Ephesians 3 : 1 8 *May you have the power to understand . . . how wide, how long, how high, and how deep his love really is.*

DRINKING

When is drinking wrong?
Ephesians 5 : 1 8 *Don't be drunk with wine, because that will ruin your life. Instead, let the Holy Spirit fill and control you.*

Exodus 3 2 : 6 *So the people got up early the next morning to sacrifice burnt offerings and peace offerings. After this, they celebrated with feasting and drinking, and indulged themselves in pagan revelry.*

Proverbs 23:29-32 *Who has anguish? Who has sorrow? Who is always fighting? Who is always complaining? Who has unnecessary bruises? Who has bloodshot eyes? It is the one who spends long hours in the taverns, trying out new drinks. Don't let the sparkle and smooth taste of wine deceive you. For in the end it bites like a poisonous serpent; it stings like a viper.* Drinking is wrong when alcohol influences our actions.

I'm addicted to drinking, and I've hurt my family. Can God help me?

2 Corinthians 5:17 *Those who become Christians become new persons. They are not the same anymore, for the old life is gone. A new life has begun!*

1 Corinthians 10:13 *Remember that the temptations that come into your life are no different from what others experience. And God is faithful. He will keep the temptation from becoming so strong that you can't stand up against it. When you are tempted, he will show you a way out so that you will not give in to it.* God is willing to help all who are trapped by addiction if they will humbly call upon him.

PROMISE FROM GOD: John 7:37-38 *Jesus stood and shouted to the crowds, "If you are thirsty, come to me! If you believe in me, come and drink! For the Scriptures declare that rivers of living water will flow out from within."*

EFFECTIVENESS

What makes us truly effective?

Genesis 39:3 *The LORD was with Joseph, giving him success in everything he did.*
Walking with God makes us effective.

2 Chronicles 26:5 *Uzziah sought God. . . . And as long as the king sought the LORD, God gave him success.*
Seeking God and relying on him makes us effective.

John 15:1-5 *I am the true vine. . . . Remain in me, and I will remain in you. For a branch cannot produce fruit if it is severed from the vine, and you cannot be fruitful apart from me. . . . Those who remain in me, and I in them, will produce much fruit. For apart from me you can do nothing.*

Romans 7:4 *Now you are united with the one who was raised from the dead. As a result, you can produce good fruit, that is, good deeds for God.*
Keeping in fellowship with, and submission to, Christ makes us effective.

Hebrews 11:33-34 *By faith these people overthrew kingdoms, ruled with justice, and received what God had promised them. They shut the mouths of lions, quenched the flames of fire, and escaped death by the edge of the sword. Their weakness was turned to strength. They became strong in battle and put whole armies to flight.*

Having strong faith in God makes us effective.

PROMISE FROM GOD: Isaiah 41:10 *Don't be afraid, for I am with you. Do not be dismayed, for I am your God. I will strengthen you. I will help you. I will uphold you with my victorious right hand.*

EMPLOYERS AND EMPLOYEES

How should an employer treat his employees?

Leviticus 19:13 *Always pay your hired workers promptly.*

Deuteronomy 24:14-15 *Never take advantage of poor laborers. . . . Pay them their wages. . . . Otherwise they might cry out to the LORD against you, and it would be counted against you as sin.*

James 5:4 *Hear the cries of the field workers whom you have cheated of their pay. The wages you held back cry out against you. The cries of the reapers have reached the ears of the Lord Almighty.*

Employers should always pay workers promptly and pay fair wages, because God is fair and expects fairness.

Ruth 2:4-5 *While she was there, Boaz arrived from Bethlehem and greeted the harvesters. "The LORD be with you!" he said. "The LORD bless you!" the harvesters replied.*

Employers should bless their workers by encouraging them and showing appreciation for what they are doing.

How should an employee respond to his employer?

2 Kings 12:15 *No accounting was required from the construction supervisors, because they were honest and faithful workers.*

Luke 16:10 *Unless you are faithful in small matters, you won't be faithful in large ones.*

Proverbs 25:13 *Faithful messengers are as refreshing as snow in the heat of summer. They revive the spirit of their employer.*

Employees should be completely faithful and honest in their work.

Proverbs 10:26 *Lazy people are a pain to their employer. They are like smoke in the eyes or vinegar that sets the teeth on edge.*

Employees should work hard for their employers.

Ecclesiastes 10:4 *If your boss is angry with you, don't quit! A quiet spirit can overcome even great mistakes.*
Even if an employer is critical and overbearing, the employee should continue to do his best and please God.

Luke 3:14 *"What should we do?" asked some soldiers. John replied, "Don't extort money, and . . . be content with your pay."*
Employees should learn to be content with their wages and not try to get more by cheating.

PROMISE FROM GOD: Proverbs 27:18 *Workers who protect their employer's interests will be rewarded.*

ENDURANCE

See PERSISTENCE

EXCUSES

Why do people make excuses for the wrong things they do?

Exodus 4:10 *Moses pleaded with the LORD, "O Lord, I'm just not a good speaker. I never have been, and I'm not now, even after you have spoken to me. I'm clumsy with words."*

Judges 6:15 *"But Lord," Gideon replied, "how can I rescue Israel? My clan is the weakest in the whole tribe of Manasseh, and I am the least in my entire family!"*

Numbers 13:31 *The other men who had explored the land with him answered, "We can't go up against them! They are stronger than we are!"*

Lack of self-confidence, which is also a lack of confidence in God, is often a reason for resistance to God's will.

Genesis 4:9 *Afterward the LORD asked Cain, "Where is your brother? Where is Abel?" "I don't know!" Cain retorted. "Am I supposed to keep track of him wherever he goes?"*

Our excuses are often a bald attempt to cover up for the wrong we have done.

1 Samuel 13:12 *So I said, "The Philistines are ready to march against us, and I haven't even asked for the LORD's help!" So I felt obliged to offer the burnt offering myself before you came.*

1 Samuel 15:15 *"It's true that the army spared the best of the sheep and cattle," Saul admitted. "But they are going to sacrifice them to the LORD your God."*

Sometimes we make excuses in order to appear pious.

Proverbs 22:13 *The lazy person is full of excuses, saying, "If I go outside, I might meet a lion in the street and be killed!"*

Laziness is at the root of some of our excuses.

Luke 9:59-61 *He said to another person, "Come, be my disciple." The man agreed, but he said, "Lord, first let me return home and bury my father." . . . Another said, "Yes, Lord, I will follow you, but first let me say good-bye to my family."*
We sometimes make excuses to cover up our lack of commitment to Christ.

How does God respond when we make excuses for our sin?

1 Samuel 15:22 *What is more pleasing to the LORD: your burnt offerings and sacrifices or your obedience to his voice? Obedience is far better than sacrifice. Listening to him is much better than offering the fat of rams.*
God sees through our pious attempts to hide our sin; he wants obedience, not hypocritical piety.

Genesis 4:10-11 *The LORD said, "What have you done? Listen—your brother's blood cries out to me from the ground! You are hereby banished from the ground you have defiled with your brother's blood."*

Matthew 25:26, 30 *The master replied, "You wicked and lazy servant! . . . Now throw this useless servant into outer darkness, where there will be weeping and gnashing of teeth."*
God will judge us for our sin if we attempt to cover it up and hide it from him.

PROMISE FROM GOD: 1 John
1 : 8 - 9 *If we say we have no sin, we are only fooling*
ourselves and refusing to accept the truth. But if we
confess our sins to him, he is faithful and just to
forgive us and to cleanse us from every wrong.

EXPECTATIONS

What should we not expect?

Esther 6 : 6 *The king said, "What should I do to*
honor a man who truly pleases me?" Haman thought
to himself, "Whom would the king wish to honor
more than me?"
We should not expect honor for ourselves, or we
might be humiliated.

Luke 13 : 26 - 27 *You will say, "But we ate and*
drank with you, and you taught in our streets." And
he will reply, "I tell you, I don't know you. Go away,
all you who do evil."
We should not expect to get into heaven by
merely knowing *about* Christ. We must know *him*
personally.

Isaiah 55 : 8 *"My thoughts are completely different*
from yours," says the LORD. "And my ways are far
beyond anything you could imagine."
We should not expect God to do things our way.

What *should* we expect?

2 Corinthians 3:8 *Shouldn't we expect far greater glory when the Holy Spirit is giving life?*

Romans 5:4-5 *Character strengthens our confident expectation of salvation. And this expectation will not disappoint us.*

Proverbs 11:23 *The godly can look forward to happiness.*
When we live for God, we can expect a glorious future.

Proverbs 11:23 *The wicked can expect only wrath.*

Hebrews 10:26-27 *Dear friends, if we deliberately continue sinning after we have received a full knowledge of the truth . . . there will be nothing to look forward to but the terrible expectation of God's judgment and the raging fire that will consume his enemies.*
When we live in rebellion against God, we should expect him to judge us.

PROMISE FROM GOD: 1 Peter 1:3-4 *Now we live with a wonderful expectation because Jesus Christ rose again from the dead. For God has reserved a priceless inheritance for his children. It is kept in heaven for you, pure and undefiled, beyond the reach of change and decay.*

FAILURE

How can I prevent failure in my life?

Matthew 7:24-27 *"Anyone who listens to my teaching and obeys me is wise, like a person who builds a house on solid rock. Though the rain comes in torrents and the floodwaters rise and the winds beat against that house, it won't collapse, because it is built on rock. But anyone who hears my teaching and ignores it is foolish, like a person who builds a house on sand. When the rains and floods come and the winds beat against that house, it will fall with a mighty crash."*
By listening to Christ and his instructions, we can avoid failure.

Joshua 8:1 *The LORD said to Joshua, "Do not be afraid or discouraged."*

1 Chronicles 28:20 *Be strong and courageous, and do the work. Don't be afraid or discouraged by the size of the task, for the LORD God . . . is with you. He will not fail you or forsake you.*
We will not fail when we put our trust completely in God and take courage in his help.

Isaiah 42:23 *Will not even one of you apply these lessons from the past and see the ruin that awaits you?*
We can avoid failure by learning from the mistakes of the past.

PROMISE FROM GOD: Psalm
37:23-24 *The steps of the godly are directed by
the LORD. He delights in every detail of their lives.
Though they stumble, they will not fall, for the LORD
holds them by the hand.*

FAIRNESS

How does God want us to treat each other fairly?

Exodus 23:2-3 *When you are on the witness
stand, do not be swayed in your testimony by the
opinion of the majority. And do not slant your
testimony in favor of a person just because that
person is poor.*

Leviticus 19:15 *Always judge your neighbors
fairly, neither favoring the poor nor showing deference
to the rich.*

We must not show favoritism; we should judge
others fairly.

Isaiah 33:15 *The ones who can live here are
those who are honest and fair, who reject making a
profit by fraud, who stay far away from bribes, who
refuse to listen to those who plot murder, who shut
their eyes to all enticement to do wrong.*

Jeremiah 22:3 *This is what the LORD says: Be fair-minded and just. Do what is right! Help those who have been robbed; rescue them from their oppressors.*
God wants us to work for justice and fairness for others.

How should I respond when life isn't fair?

Ezekiel 18:25 *"Yet you say, 'The Lord isn't being just!' Listen to me, O people of Israel. Am I the one who is unjust, or is it you?"*
We should not blame God for the unfairness of other people.

Psalm 9:8 *He will judge the world with justice and rule the nations with fairness.*

Isaiah 9:7 *His ever expanding, peaceful government will never end. He will rule forever with fairness and justice.*
Recognize that God will ultimately triumph with justice and fairness.

PROMISE FROM GOD: Psalm 37:28 *The LORD loves justice, and he will never abandon the godly. He will keep them safe forever.*

FAITH

See SALVATION

FAITHFULNESS

In what ways does God show his faithfulness to us?

Luke 1:68-70 *Praise the Lord, the God of Israel, because he has visited his people and redeemed them. He has sent us a mighty Savior from the royal line of his servant David, just as he promised through his holy prophets long ago.*

God has faithfully fulfilled his promise to send us a Savior.

Psalm 4:3 *The LORD will answer when I call to him.*

Psalm 143:1 *Hear my prayer, O LORD; listen to my plea! Answer me because you are faithful and righteous.*

When we call on God, he faithfully answers us.

1 Corinthians 1:9 *God . . . always does just what he says, and he is the one who invited you into this wonderful friendship with his Son, Jesus Christ our Lord.*

God faithfully gives us eternal life when we come to him through Christ.

What are the benefits of being faithful?

Numbers 14:24 *My servant Caleb is different from the others. He has remained loyal to me, and I will bring him into the land he explored. His descendants will receive their full share of that land.*

Faithfulness to God will be rewarded.

2 Kings 12:15 *No accounting was required from the construction supervisors, because they were honest and faithful workers.*
When we are faithful, we build a reputation for being trustworthy.

Matthew 24:45-47 *Who is a faithful, sensible servant, to whom the master can give the responsibility of managing his household and feeding his family? If the master returns and finds that the servant has done a good job, there will be a reward. . . . The master will put that servant in charge of all he owns.*
Those who are faithful with what they are given will be given even greater responsibility.

Revelation 2:10 *Remain faithful even when facing death, and I will give you the crown of life.*
Reward in heaven awaits those who are faithful to God.

PROMISE FROM GOD: Psalm 103:17-18 *The love of the LORD remains forever with those who fear him. His salvation extends to the children's children of those who are faithful to his covenant, of those who obey his commandments!*

FINISHING

Why is it important to finish what we begin?

Ecclesiastes 5:5 *It is better to say nothing than to promise something that you don't follow through on.*

Luke 14:30 *How everyone would laugh at you! They would say, "There's the person who started that building and ran out of money before it was finished!"* If we don't finish doing what we have said we would do, we hurt our reputation.

Ecclesiastes 7:8 *Finishing is better than starting. Patience is better than pride.* Following through helps us develop patience and humility in our character.

John 4:34 *Jesus explained: "My nourishment comes from doing the will of God, who sent me, and from finishing his work."*

John 17:4 *I brought glory to you here on earth by doing everything you told me to do.* When we finish what God has given us to do, we will experience blessing, and God will receive glory.

1 Corinthians 9:24 *Remember that in a race everyone runs, but only one person gets the prize. You also must run in such a way that you will win.* Those who finish are the ones who are rewarded.

Are there things which are better left unfinished?

1 Chronicles 27:24 *Joab began the census but never finished it because the anger of God broke out against Israel. The final total was never recorded in King David's official records.*

If it becomes clear that what we are doing is against God's will, then we should leave it unfinished.

Genesis 11:8 *The LORD scattered them all over the earth; and that ended the building of the city.*

We should not finish something we should never have started!

PROMISE FROM GOD:

Philippians 1:6 *God, who began the good work within you, will continue his work until it is finally finished on that day when Christ Jesus comes back again.*

FORGIVENESS

Do I have to forgive others who hurt me?

Matthew 6:14-15 *If you forgive those who sin against you, your heavenly Father will forgive you. But if you refuse to forgive others, your Father will not forgive your sins.*

We will receive God's forgiveness only when we are willing to forgive others who have wronged us.

Matthew 18:21-22 *Peter came to him and asked, "Lord, how often should I forgive someone who sins against me? Seven times?" "No!" Jesus replied, "seventy times seven!"*
Just as God forgives us without limit, we should forgive others without counting how many times.

Luke 23:34 *Jesus said, "Father, forgive these people, because they don't know what they are doing."*
Jesus forgave those who mocked him and killed him.

How do I experience forgiveness when I have done wrong?

Psalm 51:4 *Against you, and you alone, have I sinned; I have done what is evil in your sight.*
We must realize that God is the one who has been wronged by our sin.

Ezra 10:11 *Confess your sin to the LORD, the God of your ancestors, and do what he demands.*

2 Chronicles 7:14 *If my people who are called by my name will humble themselves and pray and seek my face and turn from their wicked ways, I will hear from heaven and will forgive their sins and heal their land.*

1 John 1:8-9 *If we say we have no sin, we are only fooling ourselves and refusing to accept the truth. But if we confess our sins to him, he is faithful and just to forgive us and to cleanse us from every wrong.*

We will receive God's forgiveness when we confess our sins to him, stop doing what is wrong, and turn to him with our heart.

Matthew 26:28 *This is my blood, which seals the covenant between God and his people. It is poured out to forgive the sins of many.*
Jesus died so that God's forgiveness would be freely available to us.

Acts 10:43 *Everyone who believes in him will have their sins forgiven through his name.*

Acts 13:38 *In this man Jesus there is forgiveness for your sins.*
We receive God's forgiveness by trusting in Christ.

PROMISE FROM GOD: Isaiah 43:25 *I—yes, I alone—am the one who blots out your sins for my own sake and will never think of them again.*

FRIENDSHIP

What is the mark of true friendship?
Proverbs 17:17 *A friend is always loyal, and a brother is born to help in time of need.*

1 Samuel 18:3 *Jonathan made a special vow to be David's friend.*

Some friendships are fleeting and some are lasting. True friendships are glued together with bonds of loyalty and commitment. They remain intact, despite changing external circumstances.

What gets in the way of friendships?

1 Samuel 18:9-11 *From that time on Saul kept a jealous eye on David. . . . Saul, who had a spear in his hand, suddenly hurled it at David.*
Jealousy is the great dividing force of friendships. Envy over what a friend has will soon turn to anger and bitterness, causing you to separate yourself from the one you truly cared for.

Psalm 41:9 *Even my best friend, the one I trusted completely . . . has turned against me.*
When respect or reverence is seriously damaged, even the closest friendship is at risk.

2 Samuel 13:11 *As [Tamar] was feeding [Amnon], he grabbed her and demanded, "Come to bed with me."*
Friendships are destroyed when boundaries are violated.

Genesis 50:17, 21 *"We . . . beg you to forgive us." . . . "No, don't be afraid. Indeed, I myself will take care of you."*
Forgiveness restores broken relationships.

What do I do when I'm having trouble making friends?

Job 19:19 *My close friends abhor me. Those I loved have turned against me.*

John 5:7 *I have no one to help me into the pool.*
We all go through times when it seems our friends have deserted us.

John 15:15 *I no longer call you servants. . . . Now you are my friends.*

Hebrews 13:5 *I will never fail you. I will never forsake you.*
The first thing we must do is remember that God is our constant friend and will never leave us.

Ephesians 4:32 *Be kind to each other, tenderhearted, forgiving one another, just as God through Christ has forgiven you.*
Acts of kindness and generosity attract others to you.

Does the Bible offer any guidelines for dating relationships?

1 Corinthians 13:4-5 *Love is patient and kind. Love is not jealous . . . Love does not demand its own way.*
Paul's timeless description of Christian love becomes the standard of respect and decency that should mark all our relationships, including our dating relationships.

Ephesians 5:3, 18 *Let there be no sexual immorality, impurity, or greed among you. . . . Let the Holy Spirit fill and control you.*

Matthew 5:28 *Anyone who even looks at a woman with lust in his eye has already committed adultery with her in his heart.*

In dramatic contrast to much that we see in our modern world, Jesus calls us to a standard of sexual purity in thought as well as in deed.

PROMISE FROM GOD: Matthew 18:20 *Where two or three gather together because they are mine, I am there among them.*

GAMBLING

What does God think of gambling?

Luke 12:15 *Beware! Don't be greedy for what you don't have. Real life is not measured by how much we own.*

God warns us not to be greedy.

Proverbs 10:16 *The earnings of the godly enhance their lives, but evil people squander their money on sin.*

Gambling is foolish because the money could have been put to good use.

Leviticus 16:8 *He is to cast sacred lots to determine which goat will be sacrificed to the LORD and which one will be the scapegoat.*

Numbers 34:13 *Moses told the Israelites, "This is the territory you are to divide among yourselves by sacred lot."*

Casting lots in the Bible was a method of determining God's will, not a means of making money, so it is completely different from gambling.

Are there any examples of gambling in the Bible?

Matthew 27:35 *After they had nailed him to the cross, the soldiers gambled for his clothes by throwing dice.*

The soldiers who crucified Jesus gambled to see who would get his clothes.

Why should we stay away from gambling?

Proverbs 28:22 *A greedy person tries to get rich quick, but it only leads to poverty.*

Proverbs 1:19 *Such is the fate of all who are greedy for gain. It ends up robbing them of life.*

Gambling is rooted in the hope of getting rich quick, but it often ends in poverty.

1 Thessalonians 4:11-12 *This should be your ambition: to live a quiet life, minding your own business and working with your hands. . . . As a result, people who are not Christians will respect the way you live, and you will not need to depend on others to meet your financial needs.*
Those who work for their money will be financially independent, but those who gamble often end up in financial ruin.

PROMISE FROM GOD: Ephesians 5:5 *You can be sure that no immoral, impure, or greedy person will inherit the Kingdom of Christ and of God. For a greedy person is really an idolater who worships the things of this world.*

GENEROSITY

What *is* generosity?

Deuteronomy 15:7-8 *If there are any poor people in your towns when you arrive in the land the LORD your God is giving you, do not be hard-hearted or tightfisted toward them. Instead, be generous and lend them whatever they need.*

Hebrews 13:16 *Don't forget to do good and to share what you have with those in need, for such sacrifices are very pleasing to God.*
Generosity is sharing with the needy.

Deuteronomy 16:17 *All must give as they are able, according to the blessings given to them by the LORD your God.*
Generosity involves sharing based on our blessings.

2 Corinthians 8:3 *I can testify that they gave not only what they could afford but far more. And they did it of their own free will.*

2 Corinthians 9:7 *You must each make up your own mind as to how much you should give. Don't give reluctantly or in response to pressure. For God loves the person who gives cheerfully.*
Generosity is not just *what* we give but the *attitude* with which we give it.

In what ways has God shown generosity toward us?

Romans 5:15 *What a difference between our sin and God's generous gift of forgiveness. For this one man, Adam, brought death to many through his sin. But . . . Jesus Christ, brought forgiveness to many through God's bountiful gift.*

Romans 10:12 *The . . . Lord . . . generously gives his riches to all who ask for them.*
God has generously given us forgiveness and eternal life through Christ.

Titus 3:6 *He generously poured out the Spirit upon us because of what Jesus Christ our Savior did.* God has also generously given us the Holy Spirit through Christ.

PROMISE FROM GOD: Proverbs 11:25 *The generous prosper and are satisfied; those who refresh others will themselves be refreshed.*

2 Corinthians 9:8 *God will generously provide all you need. Then you will always have everything you need and plenty left over to share with others.*

GOALS

Why is it important to have goals?

Job 6:11 *I do not have the strength to endure. I do not have a goal that encourages me to carry on.* Goals give us strength and hope.

Proverbs 4:25-27 *Look straight ahead, and fix your eyes on what lies before you. Mark out a straight path for your feet; then stick to the path and stay safe. Don't get sidetracked; keep your feet from following evil.* Goals keep us from straying into evil.

1 Corinthians 9:26 *I run straight to the goal with purpose in every step. I am not like a boxer who misses his punches.* Goals give us purpose and direction.

What kinds of goals does God want us to have?

Isaiah 26:8 *LORD, we love to obey your laws; our heart's desire is to glorify your name.*
We should pursue goals that bring glory to God.

Jeremiah 45:5 *Are you seeking great things for yourself? Don't do it!*
We should not pursue goals that bring glory to just ourselves.

Romans 14:19 *So then, let us aim for harmony in the church and try to build each other up.*

1 Corinthians 14:1 *Let love be your highest goal.*
We should make it our goal to foster harmony and love with other Christians.

James 4:4 *If your aim is to enjoy this world, you can't be a friend of God.*
Our primary goal to love God, not the pleasures of the world.

2 Corinthians 5:9 *So our aim is to please him always.*
Whatever we do, our goal should be to please God.

PROMISE FROM GOD: Psalm 37:4 *Take delight in the LORD, and he will give you your heart's desires.*

GOD'S WILL

Does God really have a plan for my life?

Psalm 139:3 *You chart the path ahead of me and tell me where to stop and rest. Every moment you know where I am.*

God cares about what we do. He cares about the details of our lives because they are a barometer of the condition of our hearts.

Psalm 138:8 *The LORD will work out his plans for my life.*

God's plans for us are always for good. Unknown plans can be frightening, but when the plans belong to God, we can rest assured that we can expect something marvelous.

Psalm 32:8 *The LORD says, "I will guide you along the best pathway for your life. I will advise you and watch over you."*

God definitely wants to help us follow the path that will be most pleasing to him, not the path that may be most pleasing to us.

What are some things I should do to discover God's will for my life?

Proverbs 2:3-5 *Cry out for insight and understanding. Search for them as you would for lost money or hidden treasure. Then you will understand what it means to fear the LORD.*

Actively look for God's will for you.

Isaiah 2:3 *Come, let us go up to the mountain of the LORD, to the Temple of the God of Israel. There he will teach us his ways, so that we may obey them.*
Let God teach you from his word.

Hosea 6:3 *Oh, that we might know the LORD! Let us press on to know him! Then he will respond to us.*
Give yourself completely to knowing his will.
Seek God's will passionately, not casually.

James 1:5 *If you want to know what God wants you to do—ask him, and he will gladly tell you. He will not resent your asking.*

Proverbs 2:6 *The LORD grants wisdom!*

1 John 5:14 *We can be confident that he will listen to us whenever we ask him for anything in line with his will.*
Pray, asking God to reveal his will to you.

Acts 21:14 *When it was clear that we couldn't persuade him, we gave up and said, "The will of the Lord be done."*
Sometimes the best way to know God's will is to let go and let God have his wonderful way. We learn more about his will for us as we allow him to work out his will in our lives.

What are some of the things we know are God's will for us?

Amos 5:24 *I want to see a mighty flood of justice, a river of righteous living that will never run dry.*
God's will is that we seek justice at all times and that we do what is right.

1 Corinthians 14:1 *Let love be your highest goal.*
God's will is that we love others.

Mark 10:45 *Even I, the Son of Man, came here not to be served but to serve others.*
God's will is that we serve others, putting them above ourselves.

Exodus 20:1 *Then God instructed the people as follows: . . .*
God's will is that we obey his laws for living.

Galatians 5:22 *When the Holy Spirit controls our lives, he will produce this kind of fruit in us.*
God's will is that we live under the power and guidance of the Holy Spirit.

Proverbs 16:3 *Commit your work to the LORD, and then your plans will succeed.*
God's will is that we do everything as if we were doing it for him.

PROMISE FROM GOD: Jeremiah 29:11 *"I know the plans I have for you," says the* LORD. *"They are plans for good and not for disaster, to give you a future and a hope."*

HABITS

How can I pass on good habits to my family?

1 Corinthians 9:25 *All athletes practice strict self-control. They do it to win a prize that will fade away, but we do it for an eternal prize.*

Deuteronomy 11:19 *Teach [God's words] to your children. Talk about them when you are at home and when you are away on a journey, when you are lying down and when you are getting up again.*

1 Timothy 4:12 *Be an example to all believers in what you teach, in the way you live, in your love, your faith, and your purity.*
When we make God part of our daily lives, we will have a more godly example to pass on.

How do we deal with bad habits?

Romans 7:15 *I don't understand myself at all, for I really want to do what is right, but I don't do it. Instead, I do the very thing I hate.*
Have you ever felt this way? Paul reveals to us one of the best ways to deal with bad habits—recognize them for what they are and confess them honestly.

1 John 2:15 *Stop loving this evil world and all that it offers you.*
Breaking a bad habit can be hard, because we are losing something we like. But losing a bad habit brings the deeper joy that we are doing what is pleasing to God.

Colossians 3:2 *Let heaven fill your thoughts.*
It will be much easier to break bad habits if we replace them with good habits.

How do we develop good habits?

Hebrews 10:25 *Let us not neglect our meeting together, as some people do.*
Meeting together as believers develops the habit of group Bible study, it keeps us busy when we might otherwise be slipping into bad habits, and it offers an accountability group.

Psalm 28:7 *The LORD is my strength, my shield from every danger. I trust in him with all my heart. . . . I burst out in songs of thanksgiving.*
As a young boy, David developed the habit of talking to God, singing songs about him, and writing psalms. This helped him to trust in and follow God all his life.

Romans 6:16 *Don't you realize that whatever you choose to obey becomes your master? You can choose sin, which leads to death, or you can choose to obey God and receive his approval.*

We daily stand at the crossroads, choosing sinful ways or God's way—the choice is ours.

PROMISE FROM GOD: Romans 8:5-6 *Those who are dominated by the sinful nature think about sinful things, but those who are controlled by the Holy Spirit think about things that please the Spirit. If your sinful nature controls your mind, there is death. But if the Holy Spirit controls your mind, there is life and peace.*

Hatred

See ANGER

Help

What kind of help will God give us when we need it?

Deuteronomy 33:29 *He is your protecting shield and your triumphant sword!*

Psalm 28:7 *The LORD is my strength, my shield from every danger. I trust in him with all my heart. He helps me, and my heart is filled with joy.*

God protects us from the enemy and gives us spiritual victory.

Isaiah 30:21 *You will hear a voice say, "This is the way; turn around and walk here."*
God guides us by his Holy Spirit.

Romans 8:26 *The Holy Spirit helps us in our distress. For we don't even know what we should pray for, nor how we should pray. But the Holy Spirit prays for us with groanings that cannot be expressed in words.*
God helps us to pray, even when we don't know how.

Genesis 2:18 *The LORD God said, "It is not good for the man to be alone. I will make a companion who will help him."*
God has given many of us a wife to help us.

In what ways should we help others?
Genesis 14:14-16 *When Abram learned that Lot had been captured, he called together the men born into his household. . . . Abram and his allies recovered everything.*
If our brother is in danger, we should do whatever we can to help him and, if necessary, to rescue him.

Acts 16:9 *That night Paul had a vision. He saw a man from Macedonia in northern Greece, pleading with him, "Come over here and help us."*
We should tell others the Good News of Christ, giving them an opportunity to be saved from judgment.

Acts 20:28 *Be sure that you feed and shepherd God's flock—his church, purchased with his blood—over whom the Holy Spirit has appointed you as elders.*
We should help other believers to grow to maturity in Christ.

Romans 12:13 *When God's children are in need, be the one to help them out. And get into the habit of inviting guests home for dinner or, if they need lodging, for the night.*
God wants us to help others by being hospitable to them in very practical ways.

Galatians 6:1 *If another Christian is overcome by some sin, you who are godly should gently and humbly help that person back onto the right path.*
When another believer has fallen into sin, we should help restore him.

PROMISE FROM GOD: Hebrews 13:6 *The Lord is my helper, so I will not be afraid. What can mere mortals do to me?*

HOLINESS

What does it mean to be holy?

2 Corinthians 6:17-18 *Come out from them and separate yourselves from them, says the Lord. Don't touch their filthy things, and I will welcome you. And I will be your Father, and you will be my sons and daughters, says the Lord Almighty.*

2 Corinthians 7:1 *Let us cleanse ourselves from everything that can defile our body or spirit. And let us work toward complete purity because we fear God.* Holiness is purity, cleanness, and separation from everything that defiles the body and the spirit.

1 Thessalonians 4:3, 7 *God wants you to be holy, so you should keep clear of all sexual sin. . . . God has called us to be holy, not to live impure lives.* Sexual purity is a necessary prerequisite for holiness.

In what ways is God holy?

Joshua 24:19 *Joshua said to the people, "You are not able to serve the LORD, for he is a holy and jealous God."*

1 Samuel 6:20 *"Who is able to stand in the presence of the LORD, this holy God?" they cried out.* God is completely separate from sin and uncleanness.

Isaiah 6:3 *Holy, holy, holy is the LORD Almighty!*
The whole earth is filled with his glory!
God is dazzling and glorious in his absolute
purity.

Amos 4:2 *The Sovereign LORD has sworn this by*
his holiness.
When God makes a promise, his holiness ensures
that he will do what he says.

Hebrews 7:26 *He is the kind of high priest we*
need because he is holy and blameless, unstained by
sin. He has now been set apart from sinners, and he
has been given the highest place of honor in heaven.
Christ is completely holy because he is
completely free from sin.

Matthew 13:41 *I, the Son of Man, will send my*
angels, and they will remove from my Kingdom
everything that causes sin and all who do evil.
God's holiness will not tolerate evil in his eternal
Kingdom.

How do we become holy?

Leviticus 21:8 *I, the LORD, am holy, and I*
make you holy.
God is the only one who can make us holy.

Job 14:4 *Who can create purity in one born*
impure? No one!
We cannot create holiness in ourselves, because
we are born in sin.

Deuteronomy 14:2 *You have been set apart as holy to the LORD your God, and he has chosen you to be his own special treasure from all the nations of the earth.*

God makes us holy by setting us apart as special for him.

Colossians 1:22 *Through his death on the cross in his own human body . . . he has brought you into the very presence of God, and you are holy and blameless as you stand before him without a single fault.*

Through Christ's death God has brought us into his presence and made us holy and blameless before him.

John 17:17 *Make them pure and holy by teaching them your words of truth.*

God makes us holy by teaching us his truth.

PROMISE FROM GOD:

1 Thessalonians 3:13 *As a result, Christ will make your hearts strong, blameless, and holy when you stand before God our Father on that day when our Lord Jesus comes with all those who belong to him.*

128

HONESTY

Why is it so important to be honest?

Psalm 24:3-4 *Who may climb the mountain of the LORD? Who may stand in his holy place? Only those whose hands and hearts are pure, who . . . never tell lies.*

To live in God's presence, we must be honest.

Proverbs 16:11 *The LORD demands fairness in every business deal; he sets the standard.*

God expects us to be honest.

Matthew 12:33 *A tree is identified by its fruit.*

Proverbs 12:5 *The plans of the godly are just.*

Luke 16:10 *If you cheat even a little, you won't be honest with greater responsibilities.*

Our level of honesty demonstrates the quality of our character.

1 Timothy 1:19 *Always keep your conscience clear. For some people have deliberately violated their consciences; as a result, their faith has been shipwrecked.*

Honesty brings a clear conscience.

Deuteronomy 25:13-15 *You must use accurate scales when you weigh out merchandise, and you must use full and honest measures . . . so that you will enjoy a long life.*

God blesses us when we are concerned more about treating others fairly than about how much we get for ourselves.

PROMISE FROM GOD: Psalm 37:37 *Look at those who are honest and good, for a wonderful future lies before those who love peace.*

HOPE

So where does hope come from?

Psalm 39:7 *Lord, where do I put my hope? My only hope is in you.*

The Lord himself is the source of hope, because he determines our future.

Why should I trust God as my hope?

Hebrews 6:18 *God has given us both his promise and his oath. These two things are unchangeable because it is impossible for God to lie.*

Hebrews 10:23 *God can be trusted to keep his promise.*

God cannot lie because he *is* truth. God, therefore, cannot break his promises. His word stands forever.

1 Peter 1:21 *Because God raised Christ from the dead and gave him great glory, your faith and hope can be placed confidently in God.*

God has proven his power over everything, and by this power he keeps his promises.

How can I have hope in what seems a hopeless situation?

Psalm 18:4-6 *The ropes of death surrounded me; the floods of destruction swept over me. The grave wrapped its ropes around me; death itself stared me in the face. But in my distress I cried out to the LORD; yes, I prayed to my God for help. He heard me from his sanctuary; my cry reached his ears.*

Hope is trusting God to act in his good timing. Hope also means carrying with us an eternal perspective that realizes sin and evil may sometimes thwart our plans here on earth but never God's plans in heaven.

PROMISE FROM GOD: Jeremiah 29:11 *"For I know the plans I have for you," says the LORD. "They are plans for good and not for disaster, to give you a future and a hope."*

HUMILITY

What is true humility?

Zephaniah 3:12 *Those who are left will be the lowly and the humble, for it is they who trust in the name of the LORD.*

Humility is not thinking too highly of yourself.

Matthew 18:4 *Anyone who becomes as humble as this little child is the greatest in the Kingdom of Heaven.*
Humility is childlikeness.

Psalm 51:3-4 *I recognize my shameful deeds. . . . Against you, and you alone, have I sinned; I have done what is evil in your sight. You will be proved right in what you say, and your judgment against me is just.*
Humility involves the willingness to confess sin.

How was Jesus humble?

Zechariah 9:9 *Look, your king is coming to you. He is righteous and victorious, yet he is humble, riding on a donkey—even on a donkey's colt.*
Jesus is King of kings, yet in his royal procession he rode on a donkey.

Philippians 2:6-8 *Though he was God, he did not demand and cling to his rights as God. He made himself nothing; he took the humble position of a slave and appeared in human form. And in human form he obediently humbled himself even further by dying a criminal's death on a cross.*
Jesus is God, yet he made himself nothing and suffered death on the cross for us.

Matthew 11:29 *Take my yoke upon you. Let me teach you, because I am humble and gentle, and you will find rest for your souls.*

Jesus is the ultimate role model of gentleness and humility.

How do I become humble?

Deuteronomy 8:2-3 *Remember how the LORD your God led you through the wilderness for forty years. . . . He humbled you by letting you go hungry and then feeding you with manna. . . . He did it to teach you that people need more than bread for their life.*

Humility comes when we recognize that we need God and that God is the one who meets our needs.

1 Peter 3:8 *Finally, all of you should be of one mind, full of sympathy toward each other, loving one another with tender hearts and humble minds.*

Humility comes from developing sympathetic and tender hearts toward others.

1 Peter 5:5 *All of you, serve each other in humility, for "God sets himself against the proud, but he shows favor to the humble."*

Serving other people will develop humility in us.

How does God respond to the humble?

Psalm 25:9 *He leads the humble in what is right, teaching them his way.*

God leads and teaches the humble.

1 Peter 5:6 *Humble yourselves under the mighty power of God, and in his good time he will honor you.*
The Lord honors the humble.

Daniel 10:12 *He said, "Don't be afraid, Daniel. Since the first day you began to pray for understanding and to humble yourself before your God, your request has been heard in heaven. I have come in answer to your prayer."*
God acknowledges the prayers of the humble.

Psalm 69:32 *The humble will see their God at work and be glad. Let all who seek God's help live in joy.*
Humility opens our eyes to see God at work in our lives.

PROMISE FROM GOD: Matthew 23:12 *Those who exalt themselves will be humbled, and those who humble themselves will be exalted.*

HURRY

When should we hurry?

Genesis 19:14-15 *Lot rushed out to tell his daughters' fiancés, "Quick, get out of the city! The LORD is going to destroy it." . . . At dawn the next morning the angels became insistent. "Hurry," they said to Lot. "Take your wife and your two daughters who are here. Get out of here right now, or you will be caught in the destruction of the city."*

We should hurry when we need to get out of harm's way.

1 Samuel 25:18, 32-34 *Abigail lost no time. She quickly gathered two hundred loaves of bread, two skins of wine, five dressed sheep, nearly a bushel of roasted grain, one hundred raisin cakes, and two hundred fig cakes. . . . David replied to Abigail, ". . . I swear by the LORD, the God of Israel, who has kept me from hurting you, that if you had not hurried out to meet me, not one of Nabal's men would be alive tomorrow morning."*

Matthew 5:25 *Come to terms quickly with your enemy before it is too late and you are dragged into court, handed over to an officer, and thrown in jail.* When someone else has something against us, we should hurry to be reconciled with them.

Psalm 119:60 *I will hurry, without lingering, to obey your commands.*

John 9:4 *All of us must quickly carry out the tasks assigned us by the one who sent me, because there is little time left before the night falls and all work comes to an end.* We should hurry to obey God.

When is hurrying unwise?

Joshua 8:14 *When the king of Ai saw the Israelites across the valley, he and all his army hurriedly went out early the next morning and attacked the Israelites at a place overlooking the Jordan Valley. But he didn't realize there was an ambush behind the city.*

When we hurry to act without checking our assumptions, we may make very serious mistakes.

Judges 11:31 *I will give to the LORD the first thing coming out of my house to greet me when I return in triumph. I will sacrifice it as a burnt offering.*

Ecclesiastes 5:2 *Don't make rash promises to God, for he is in heaven, and you are only here on earth. So let your words be few.*

We should think carefully before rushing to making promises.

Proverbs 13:3 *Those who control their tongue will have a long life; a quick retort can ruin everything.*

Proverbs 14:29 *Those who control their anger have great understanding; those with a hasty temper will make mistakes.*

James 1:19 *My dear brothers and sisters, be quick to listen, slow to speak, and slow to get angry.*

We should be in no hurry to respond to others with angry words.

Proverbs 19:2 *Zeal without knowledge is not good; a person who moves too quickly may go the wrong way.*
It is better to plan carefully than to move too quickly.

PROMISE FROM GOD: Proverbs 21:5 *Good planning and hard work lead to prosperity, but hasty shortcuts lead to poverty.*

Isaiah 52:12 *You will not leave in a hurry, running for your lives. For the LORD will go ahead of you, and the God of Israel will protect you from behind.*

HYPOCRISY

What does God think about hypocrisy?

Psalm 50:16-17 *Recite my laws no longer, and don't pretend that you obey me. For you refuse my discipline and treat my laws like trash.*
God is angry when evil people pretend to be good.

Proverbs 28:9 *The prayers of a person who ignores the law are despised.*

Isaiah 1:15 *From now on, when you lift up your hands in prayer, I will refuse to look. Even though you offer many prayers, I will not listen. For your hands are covered with the blood of your innocent victims.*

Amos 5:21 *I hate all your show and pretense—the hypocrisy of your religious festivals and solemn assemblies.*

God hates religious hypocrisy.

Isaiah 29:13 *The Lord says, "These people say they are mine. They honor me with their lips, but their hearts are far away. And their worship of me amounts to nothing more than human laws learned by rote."*

God sees through people's hypocrisy.

How should I respond when others are hypocritical?

Psalm 26:4 *I do not spend time with liars or go along with hypocrites.*

Don't spend lots of time with obviously hypocritical people because it is so easy to pick up their habits.

Galatians 2:11 *When Peter came to Antioch, I had to oppose him publicly, speaking strongly against what he was doing, for it was very wrong.*

When our brothers in Christ are acting hypocritically, sometimes a public confrontation is necessary.

How do I avoid being a hypocrite?

Matthew 5:23-24 *If you are standing before the altar in the Temple, offering a sacrifice to God, and you suddenly remember that someone has something against you, leave your sacrifice there beside the altar. Go and be reconciled to that person. Then come and offer your sacrifice to God.*
We should take care of any wrong in our life before worshiping God publicly.

James 3:17 *The wisdom that comes from heaven is first of all pure. . . . It is full of mercy and good deeds. It shows no partiality and is always sincere.*
We need God's Spirit to give us true sincerity.

James 4:8 *Draw close to God, and God will draw close to you. Wash your hands, you sinners; purify your hearts, you hypocrites.*
Drawing near to God will help us get rid of hypocrisy in our lives.

PROMISE FROM GOD: Ezekiel 14:10 *False prophets and hypocrites—evil people who claim to want my advice—will all be punished for their sins.*

IDOLATRY

What is idolatry?

Exodus 20:1-5 *Then God instructed the people as follows: "I am the LORD your God, who rescued you from slavery in Egypt. Do not worship any other gods besides me. Do not make idols of any kind, whether in the shape of birds or animals or fish. You must never worship or bow down to them, for I, the LORD your God, am a jealous God who will not share your affection with any other god!"*
Idolatry is worshiping anything other than the Lord himself.

Isaiah 44:17 *Then he takes what's left and makes his god: a carved idol! He falls down in front of it, worshiping and praying to it. "Rescue me!" he says. "You are my god!"*
Idolatry is trusting anything other than the Lord for salvation.

1 John 5:21 *Dear children, keep away from anything that might take God's place in your hearts.*
An idol is anything that takes God's place in our hearts.

What kinds of idols do people worship today?

Leviticus 19:4 *Do not . . . make gods of metal for yourselves.*

People may not often make statues, but many people worship man-made objects.

Deuteronomy 4:15-18 *Be careful! You did not see the LORD's form on the day he spoke to you from the fire at Mount Sinai. So do not corrupt yourselves by making a physical image in any form—whether of a man or a woman, an animal or a bird, a creeping creature or a fish.*

Even today some people worship pictures, not knowing that it is idolatry.

Deuteronomy 4:19 *When you look up into the sky and see the sun, moon, and stars—all the forces of heaven—don't be seduced by them and worship them. The LORD your God designated these heavenly bodies for all the peoples of the earth.*

Romans 1:21-25 *Yes, they knew God, but they wouldn't worship him as God or even give him thanks. . . . And instead of worshiping the glorious, ever-living God, . . . they worshiped the things God made but not the Creator himself.*

Many people worship the creation rather than God himself, the Creator.

2 Chronicles 33:6 *Manasseh . . . practiced sorcery, divination, and witchcraft, and he consulted with mediums and psychics. He did much that was evil in the LORD's sight, arousing his anger.*

Some worship spiritual powers which are not from God.

Acts 10:25-26 *As Peter entered his home, Cornelius fell to the floor before him in worship. But Peter pulled him up and said, "Stand up! I'm a human being like you!"*

Acts 14:11-15 *When the listening crowd saw what Paul had done, they shouted in their local dialect, "These men are gods in human bodies!"* Many people make the mistake of worshiping celebrities and other impressive figures.

Colossians 2:18 *Don't let anyone say you must worship angels, even though they say they have had visions about this.*
Some people revere their own spiritual experiences.

PROMISE FROM GOD: Jeremiah 10:11 *Say this to those who worship other gods: "Your so-called gods, who did not make the heavens and earth, will vanish from the earth."*

Ezekiel 36:25 *Then I will sprinkle clean water on you, and you will be clean. Your filth will be washed away, and you will no longer worship idols.*

INTEGRITY

See CHARACTER and HONESTY

INTIMACY

What is the basis for true and lasting intimacy in marriage?

Proverbs 5:15-19 *Drink water from your own well—share your love only with your wife. . . . May you always be captivated by her love.*

Proverbs 18:22 *The man who finds a wife finds a treasure.*

Proverbs 31:10-11 *Who can find a virtuous and capable wife? She is worth more than precious rubies. Her husband can trust her, and she will greatly enrich his life.*

1 Corinthians 7:3 *The husband should not deprive his wife of sexual intimacy, which is her right as a married woman.*

Ephesians 5:24-25 *You husbands must love your wives with the same love Christ showed the church. He gave up his life for her.*

True and lasting intimacy in marriage is based on: (1) faithfulness, (2) rejoicing in one another, (3) letting each satisfy the other in love and sexuality, and (4) loving your wife as Christ loved the church and died for it.

What must I do to experience an intimate relationship with God?

Genesis 6:9 *Noah was a righteous man, the only blameless man living on earth at the time. He consistently followed God's will and enjoyed a close relationship with him.*

We must live the way God wants us to live.

Psalm 27:8 *My heart has heard you say, "Come and talk with me." And my heart responds, "LORD, I am coming."*

Psalm 145:18 *The LORD is close to all who call on him, yes, to all who call on him sincerely.*

If we are to have a close relationship with God, we must talk with him.

James 4:8 *Draw close to God, and God will draw close to you. Wash your hands, you sinners; purify your hearts, you hypocrites.*

Drawing close to God and purifying our hearts before him is necessary for intimacy with him.

Exodus 34:14 *You must worship no other gods, but only the LORD, for he is a God who is passionate about his relationship with you.*

We must worship God only.

Romans 5:11 *We can rejoice in our wonderful new relationship with God—all because of what our Lord Jesus Christ has done for us in making us friends of God.*

When we put our trust in Christ, God makes us his friends.

PROMISE FROM GOD:
1 Chronicles 28:9 *If you seek him, you will find him.*

JEALOUSY

Why is our jealousy so dangerous?
Proverbs 14:30 *A relaxed attitude lengthens life; jealousy rots it away.*
Jealousy brings decay to our lives because it causes us to focus on anger and bitterness.

Proverbs 27:4 *Anger is cruel . . . but who can survive the destructiveness of jealousy?*

Genesis 13:7 *An argument broke out between the herdsmen of Abram and Lot.*
Jealousy tears families and friends apart. Jealousy drove Lot's herdsmen to fight with his uncle Abram's herdsmen.

What does it mean that God is "a jealous God"?
Exodus 34:14 *You must worship no other gods, but only the LORD, for he is a God who is passionate about his relationship with you.*

Deuteronomy 5:9 *I, the LORD your God, am a jealous God who will not share your affection with any other god!*

Deuteronomy 32:21 *They have roused my jealousy by worshiping nongods.*

Zechariah 1:14 *This is what the LORD Almighty says: My love for Jerusalem and Mount Zion is passionate and strong.*

When people give their honor, praise, and love to other things, God is jealous because the honor due him has been squandered elsewhere. Because God deserves all our honor, praise, and love, this is an honest recognition of what he deserves.

Where does jealousy take us? What can happen next?

Proverbs 12:12 *Thieves are jealous of each other's loot, while the godly bear their own fruit.*

Thieves steal from others in response to their jealousy and lust for someone else's money. Generous people, on the other hand, love to give, and that becomes their driving force in life.

Genesis 4:4-5 *The LORD accepted Abel's offering, but he did not accept Cain's. This made Cain very angry.*

Galatians 5:22 *When the Holy Spirit controls our lives, he will produce this kind of fruit in us.*

When we seek the character traits that come from the Holy Spirit, we are spared from petty human jealousy and the hard feelings that come from the competition for honor and popularity.

PROMISE FROM GOD: Mark 11:24-25 *Listen to me! You can pray for anything, and if you believe, you will have it. But when you are praying, first forgive anyone you are holding a grudge against, so that your Father in heaven will forgive your sins, too.*

JUDGING OTHERS

What does God think of our judging others?

1 Corinthians 4:5 *Be careful not to jump to conclusions before the Lord returns as to whether or not someone is faithful. When the Lord comes, he will bring our deepest secrets to light and will reveal our private motives. And then God will give to everyone whatever praise is due.*

We should be very slow to judge others, because only God is capable of judging rightly every time.

Romans 2:1 *You may be saying, "What terrible people you have been talking about!" But you are just as bad, and you have no excuse! When you say they are wicked and should be punished, you are condemning yourself, for you do these very same things.*

When we condemn others for their sin, God sees our hypocrisy.

1 Samuel 16:7 *The LORD said to Samuel, "Don't judge by his appearance or height, for I have rejected him. The LORD doesn't make decisions the way you do! People judge by outward appearance, but the LORD looks at a person's thoughts and intentions."* God doesn't want us to make judgments based on outward appearance.

Leviticus 19:15 *Always judge your neighbors fairly, neither favoring the poor nor showing deference to the rich.*
When we have to make a judgment, we must do so with fairness and integrity.

What are the consequences of judging others?

2 Samuel 12:5-7 *David was furious. "As surely as the LORD lives," he vowed, "any man who would do such a thing deserves to die! He must repay four lambs to the poor man for the one he stole and for having no pity." Then Nathan said to David, "You are that man!"*
If we are too quick to judge others, we may be found guilty of the same things.

Matthew 7:2 *Others will treat you as you treat them. Whatever measure you use in judging others, it will be used to measure how you are judged.*

Luke 6:37 *Stop criticizing others, or it will all come back on you. If you forgive others, you will be forgiven.*
We will be judged by the same standard we use.

PROMISE FROM GOD:
Ecclesiastes 12:14 *God will judge us for everything we do, including every secret thing, whether good or bad.*

Matthew 7:1 *Stop judging others, and you will not be judged.*

LEADERSHIP

What are some keys to effective leadership?

Genesis 12:1, 4 *The LORD told Abram, "Leave your country, your relatives, and your father's house, and go to the land that I will show you. . . ." Abram departed as the LORD had instructed him, and Lot went with him.*

1 Kings 22:14 *As surely as the LORD lives, I will say only what the LORD tells me to say.*
A good leader follows the Lord's leadership.

Numbers 20:12 *The LORD said to Moses and Aaron, "Because you did not trust me enough to demonstrate my holiness to the people of Israel, you will not lead them into the land I am giving them!"*

Godly leaders demonstrate God's character through their leadership.

Deuteronomy 1:12-13 *How can I settle all your quarrels and problems by myself? Choose some men from each tribe who have wisdom, understanding, and a good reputation, and I will appoint them as your leaders.*

A wise leader delegates some of his responsibilities to trustworthy subordinates.

Deuteronomy 31:7 *Be strong and courageous! For you will lead these people into the land that the LORD swore to give their ancestors.*

Nehemiah 2:20 *The God of heaven will help us succeed.*

Leaders should lead with righteousness and justice.

Nehemiah 5:9 *I pressed further, "What you are doing is not right!"*

Courageous leaders stand up to those who are doing what is wrong.

Luke 22:25-26 *Jesus told them, "In this world the kings and great men order their people around, and yet they are called 'friends of the people.' But among you, those who are the greatest should take the lowest rank, and the leader should be like a servant."*

Christlike leaders lead by serving, not by ordering others around.

Hebrews 2:10 *Through the suffering of Jesus, God made him a perfect leader, one fit to bring them into their salvation.*

A truly effective leader will be acquainted with difficulty and suffering.

How do we know if and when we should exercise leadership?

Deuteronomy 3:28 *Commission Joshua and encourage him, for he will lead the people across the Jordan. He will give them the land you now see before you.*

If you have been commissioned to lead, then lead!

Ezekiel 3:17 *Son of man, I have appointed you as a watchman for Israel. Whenever you receive a message from me, pass it on to the people immediately.*

John 15:16 *You didn't choose me. I chose you. I appointed you to go and produce fruit that will last.*

You don't need to have an official position to lead, but God's calling is essential.

PROMISE FROM GOD: Proverbs 29:14 *A king who is fair to the poor will have a long reign.*

Jeremiah 3:15 *I will give you leaders after my own heart, who will guide you with knowledge and understanding.*

LEISURE

Does God want us to have leisure?

Leviticus 23:3 *You may work for six days each week, but on the seventh day all work must come to a complete stop. It is the LORD's Sabbath day of complete rest, a holy day to assemble for worship. It must be observed wherever you live.*

Isaiah 58:13 *Keep the Sabbath day holy. Don't pursue your own interests on that day, but enjoy the Sabbath and speak of it with delight as the LORD's holy day. Honor the LORD in everything you do, and don't follow your own desires or talk idly.*

God wants us to have total rest one day in seven.

Matthew 11:28-30 *Jesus said, "Come to me, all of you who are weary and carry heavy burdens, and I will give you rest. Take my yoke upon you. Let me teach you, because I am humble and gentle, and you will find rest for your souls. For my yoke fits perfectly, and the burden I give you is light."*

Jesus gives us true spiritual rest when we come to him.

Mark 6:31 *Jesus said, "Let's get away from the crowds for a while and rest." There were so many people coming and going that Jesus and his apostles didn't even have time to eat.*

All of us need time away periodically for rest and refreshment.

What kinds of leisure are unnecessary and harmful?

Psalm 73:12 *Look at these arrogant people—enjoying a life of ease while their riches multiply.*

2 Thessalonians 3:6 *Stay away from any Christian who lives in idleness and doesn't follow the tradition of hard work we gave you.*
While times of leisure are necessary, God doesn't want us to make leisure the center of our lifestyle.

Proverbs 12:11 *Hard work means prosperity; only fools idle away their time.*
It is foolish to waste time in the name of leisure.

Isaiah 47:8 *You are a pleasure-crazy kingdom, living at ease and feeling secure, bragging as if you were the greatest in the world!*
Living for pleasure is a big mistake.

PROMISE FROM GOD: Hebrews 4:9-10 *There is a special rest still waiting for the people of God. For all who enter into God's rest will find rest from their labors, just as God rested after creating the world.*

LIMITATIONS

Does God have any limitations?

Numbers 11:23 *The LORD said to Moses, "Is there any limit to my power? Now you will see whether or not my word comes true!"*

Isaiah 40:28 *Have you never heard or understood? Don't you know that the LORD is the everlasting God, the Creator of all the earth? He never grows faint or weary.*

There is no limitation to God's power and strength.

Psalm 139:1-12 *O LORD, you have examined my heart and know everything about me. . . . You know what I am going to say even before I say it, LORD. . . . I can never escape from your spirit! I can never get away from your presence! . . . To you the night shines as bright as day. Darkness and light are both alike to you.*

Isaiah 40:28 *No one can measure the depths of his understanding.*

God's knowledge has no limit, and there is no place where he is not.

What limitations do we have?

Numbers 11:14 *I can't carry all these people by myself! The load is far too heavy!*

Even the greatest men can't do everything.

Job 14:1 *How frail is humanity! How short is life, and how full of trouble!*

Psalm 103:16 *The wind blows, and we are gone—as though we had never been here.*

1 Peter 1:24 *People are like grass that dies away; their beauty fades as quickly as the beauty of wildflowers. The grass withers, and the flowers fall away.*
We are limited by our physical frailty and by our mortality.

Ecclesiastes 8:7 *Indeed, how can people avoid what they don't know is going to happen?*
We are unable to see the future, which places severe limitations on us.

Matthew 26:40 *He returned to the disciples and found them asleep. He said to Peter, "Couldn't you stay awake and watch with me even one hour?"*

Romans 7:18 *I know I am rotten through and through so far as my old sinful nature is concerned. No matter which way I turn, I can't make myself do right. I want to, but I can't.*
The weakness of our flesh limits us.

PROMISE FROM GOD: Ephesians 3:20 *Glory be to God! By his mighty power at work within us, he is able to accomplish infinitely more than we would ever dare to ask or hope.*

LISTENING

Why is listening so important?

Proverbs 1:9 *What you learn from them will crown you with grace and clothe you with honor.*
Listening helps us grow and mature.

Proverbs 5:13 *Oh, why didn't I listen to my teachers? Why didn't I pay attention to those who gave me instruction?*
Listening helps keep us accountable.

Proverbs 2:1-9 *My child, listen to me. . . . Then . . . you will know how to find the right course of action every time.*
Listening is essential to good decision making.

Proverbs 8:6 *Listen to me! For I have excellent things to tell you.*
Listening gives us the opportunity to hear excellent things.

Exodus 18:24 *Moses listened to his father-in-law's advice and followed his suggestions.*

Job 29:21 *Everyone listened to me and valued my advice.*
Listening shows that we respect others. It honors the words of others. There is something affirming about feeling that you've been listened to.

Proverbs 21:13 *Those who shut their ears to the cries of the poor will be ignored in their own time of need.*

Listening is more than hearing; it's a connecting with others. It helps us know where they are coming from.

What are some things we shouldn't listen to?

Genesis 3:6 *The fruit looked so fresh and delicious. . . . So she ate some.*

Matthew 6:13 *Don't let us yield to temptation.*
Temptation

Leviticus 19:16 *Do not spread slanderous gossip among your people.*
Gossip

2 Peter 2:1 *There were also false prophets in Israel, just as there will be false teachers among you.*

Mark 13:21 *If anyone tells you, "Look, here is the Messiah," or, "There he is," don't pay any attention.*
False teaching

Ephesians 5:4 *Obscene stories, foolish talk, and coarse jokes—these are not for you.*

Proverbs 12:18 *Some people make cutting remarks, but the words of the wise bring healing.*
Insults and off-color stories

Proverbs 13:5 *Those who are godly hate lies.*
Lies

Proverbs 29:5 *To flatter people is to lay a trap for their feet.*
Flattery

How do we listen to God?

Psalm 4:3 *You can be sure of this. . . . The LORD will answer when I call to him.*

Psalm 5:3 *Each morning I bring my requests to you and wait expectantly.*
Prayer is a two-way conversation: we speak to God, and God speaks to us.

Psalm 46:10 *Be silent, and know that I am God!*
Quietness helps us hear God's voice.

1 Kings 19:12 *After the earthquake, there was a fire, but the LORD was not in the fire. And after the fire there was the sound of a gentle whisper.*
God is big, so we expect him to speak with the voice of thunder or lightning or earthquake or fire. But God often expresses his powerful love in gentle whispers. Listen for God's whispers as well as his shouts.

PROMISE FROM GOD: Proverbs 1:23 *Come here and listen to me! I'll pour out the spirit of wisdom upon you and make you wise.*

LOVE

Must I love other people? What if I don't want to?

John 13:34 *I now am giving you a new commandment: Love each other. Just as I have loved you, you should love each other.*

1 John 2:9 *Anyone who says, "I am in the light" but rejects another Christian is still in darkness.*

John 13:35 *Your love for one another will prove to the world that you are my disciples.*

1 Peter 4:8 *Love covers a multitude of sins.*

1 John 4:12 *If we love each other, God lives in us, and his love has been brought to full expression through us.*
God expects Christians to love others. Our conduct is proof of whether we love each other, and loving each other is proof that we belong to Christ.

What are some special things that come from a loving relationship?

Proverbs 10:12 *Hatred stirs up quarrels, but love covers all offenses.*

1 Corinthians 13:4-7 *Love is patient and kind. Love is not jealous or boastful or proud or rude. Love does not demand its own way. Love is not irritable, and it keeps no record of when it has been wronged. It is never glad about injustice but rejoices whenever the truth wins out. Love never gives up, never loses faith, is always hopeful, and endures through every circumstance.*

Love is expressed in many ways, including: (1) forgiveness, (2) patience, (3) kindness, (4) love for truth, (5) love for justice, (6) love for the best in a person, (7) loyalty at any cost, (8) belief in a person no matter what. Love does not allow for (1) jealousy, (2) envy, (3) pride, (4) a haughty spirit, (5) selfishness, (6) rudeness, (7) a demand for one's own way, (8) irritability, (9) grudges.

Does God really love me? How can I know?

Hosea 2:19 *I will make you my wife forever, showing you righteousness and justice, unfailing love and compassion.*

John 3:16 *God so loved the world that he gave his only Son, so that everyone who believes in him will not perish but have eternal life.*

1 John 4:9-10 *God showed how much he loved us by sending his only Son into the world so that we might have eternal life through him. This is real love.*

Romans 5:5 *[God] has given us the Holy Spirit to fill our hearts with his love.*

Romans 8:38 *Nothing can ever separate us from his love.*

How should we show our love to God?

Matthew 10:42 *If you give even a cup of cold water to one of the least of my followers, you will surely be rewarded.*
By showing our love to needy people whom God loves

John 14:21 *Those who obey my commandments are the ones who love me.*
By obeying him

John 21:15-17 *Do you love me? . . . Feed my lambs. . . . Take care of my sheep. . . . Feed my sheep.*

Hebrews 6:10 *He will not forget . . . how you have shown your love to him by caring for other Christians.*
By guiding and helping Jesus' followers

Psalm 122:1 *I was glad when they said to me, "Let us go to the house of the LORD."*
By worshiping him and praising him for his love to us

PROMISE FROM GOD: Romans 8:39 *Whether we are high above the sky or in the deepest ocean, nothing in all creation will ever be able to separate us from the love of God that is revealed in Christ Jesus our Lord.*

LUST

If lust does not involve actual physical behavior, why is it wrong?

Luke 11:34 *Your eye is a lamp for your body. A pure eye lets sunshine into your soul.*

When lust is allowed to take up residence in our minds, it tends to consume our thoughts and push the light of God aside.

1 Kings 11:3 *He had seven hundred wives and three hundred concubines. And sure enough, they led his heart away from the LORD.*

Solomon's lust led not only to promiscuity but to his turning away from God.

What is the difference between lust and love?

2 Samuel 13:14 *Amnon wouldn't listen to [Tamar], and since he was stronger than she was, he raped her.*

Love does not take what is not offered. Lust takes what it wants, regardless of the other's needs or desires.

1 Corinthians 13:4-5 *Love is patient and kind. . . . Love does not demand its own way.*
Love is patient and kind. Lust is impatient and rude.

How can I keep my desires from becoming lust?

Matthew 5:28 *Anyone who even looks at a woman with lust in his eye has already committed adultery with her in his heart.*
We can prevent lust from taking root in our minds by avoiding that "second look."

Philippians 4:8 *Think about things that are pure and lovely and admirable.*
When we fill our hearts and minds with purity and goodness, lust finds no place to dwell.

Song of Songs 7:6 *Oh, how delightful you are, my beloved; how pleasant for utter delight!*
God created us to experience the joys of sexual intimacy within the bonds of marriage. Song of Songs reminds us that our pleasure is truly fulfilling only when pursued in harmony with God's plan.

Is it possible to lust for something other than physical pleasure?

Job 22:24 *Give up your lust for money, and throw your precious gold into the river.*

Exodus 20:17 *Do not covet your neighbor's house.*
There are many things that we "lust" for. Power,
wealth, and material things all can become
objects of our lust.

PROMISE FROM GOD: James
1:14-15 *Temptation comes from the lure of our
own evil desires. These evil desires lead to evil actions,
and evil actions lead to death.*

LYING

See DECEIT and HONESTY

MATERIALISM

Why should we avoid materialism?

Deuteronomy 7:25 *You must burn their idols
in fire, and do not desire the silver or gold with which
they are made. Do not take it or it will become a
snare to you.*

Matthew 6:21 *Wherever your treasure is, there
your heart and thoughts will also be.*
Materialism turns us away from worshiping the Lord.

Genesis 14:12 *They also captured Lot—Abram's
nephew who lived in Sodom—and took everything he
owned.*
Materialism makes us vulnerable to the enemy.

Ecclesiastes 5:10 *Those who love money will never have enough. How absurd to think that wealth brings true happiness!*
Material things never bring the happiness they promise.

Matthew 6:19 *Don't store up treasures here on earth, where they can be eaten by moths and get rusty, and where thieves break in and steal.*
Material things get rusty and stolen.

Mark 4:19 *All too quickly the message is crowded out by the cares of this life, the lure of wealth, and the desire for nice things, so no crop is produced.*
Materialism keeps us from producing spiritual fruit.

How do I get rid of materialism in my life?

Genesis 45:20 *Don't worry about your belongings, for the best of all the land of Egypt is yours.*
Stop worry about belongings and start trusting God to provide.

Job 1:21 *I came naked from my mother's womb, and I will be stripped of everything when I die. The LORD gave me everything I had, and the LORD has taken it away. Praise the name of the LORD!*
Always remember that everything comes from the hand of God, and everything is God's.

Psalm 4:7 *You have given me greater joy than those who have abundant harvests of grain and wine.* Realize that joy and satisfaction come from God, not from having possessions.

Matthew 6:20 *Store your treasures in heaven, where they will never become moth-eaten or rusty and where they will be safe from thieves.*

Colossians 3:2-3 *Let heaven fill your thoughts. Do not think only about things down here on earth. For you died when Christ died, and your real life is hidden with Christ in God.* Redirect your focus from material things to things that will last forever, such as God and his truth.

Luke 16:9 *I tell you, use your worldly resources to benefit others and make friends. In this way, your generosity stores up a reward for you in heaven.* Focus your efforts on helping others rather than on acquiring more.

PROMISE FROM GOD: 1 John 2:17 *This world is fading away, along with everything it craves. But if you do the will of God, you will live forever.*

MEEKNESS

How can meekness be a masculine trait?

Exodus 32:19-20 *Moses saw the calf and the dancing. In terrible anger, he threw the stone tablets to the ground, smashing them at the foot of the mountain. He took the calf they had made and melted it in the fire. And when the metal had cooled, he ground it into powder and mixed it with water. Then he made the people drink it.*

Numbers 12:3 *Moses was more humble than any other person on earth.*

Moses was one of the greatest and strongest leaders ever, yet he was truly meek.

2 Samuel 16:9-12 *"Why should this dead dog curse my lord the king?" Abishai son of Zeruiah demanded. "Let me go over and cut off his head!" "No!" the king said. . . . "Leave him alone and let him curse, for the LORD has told him to do it. And perhaps the LORD will see that I am being wronged and will bless me because of these curses."*

David, the powerful warrior and king, was truly meek, as demonstrated by his response to criticism.

Proverbs 16:32 *It is better to be patient than powerful; it is better to have self-control than to conquer a city.*
Patience and self-control—elements of meekness—demonstrate true inner strength.

How do I exercise meekness in my life?

Proverbs 15:1 *A gentle answer turns away wrath, but harsh words stir up anger.*
Answer anger with gentleness.

Luke 6:28-29 *Pray for the happiness of those who curse you. Pray for those who hurt you. If someone slaps you on one cheek, turn the other cheek. If someone demands your coat, offer your shirt also.*
Praying for our enemies and doing good for them will help us learn meekness.

PROMISE FROM GOD: Psalm 37:11 *Those who are gentle and lowly will possess the land; they will live in prosperous security.*

Matthew 5:5 *God blesses those who are gentle and lowly, for the whole earth will belong to them.*

MONEY

What is a proper perspective toward money?

Psalm 23:1 *The LORD is my shepherd; I have everything I need.*

Matthew 6:24 *No one can serve two masters. . . . You cannot serve both God and money.*
The love of money can get our priorities out of line. We must keep reminding ourselves that God must be first in our lives and that money cannot satisfy our deepest needs.

1 Timothy 6:10 *The love of money is at the root of all kinds of evil.*

Hebrews 13:5 *Stay away from the love of money; be satisfied with what you have. For God has said, "I will never fail you. I will never forsake you."*

Psalm 119:36 *Give me an eagerness for your decrees; do not inflict me with love for money!*
Money is not the root of all evil; the love of it is!

Proverbs 11:28 *Trust in your money and down you go!*

Isaiah 55:2 *Why spend your money on food that does not give you strength? . . . Listen, and I will tell you where to get food that is good for the soul!*

Too often we buy things to fill a void or a need in our lives. The Bible points to a way to acquire a deep and lasting happiness that always satisfies.

Proverbs 19:1 *It is better to be poor and honest than to be a fool and dishonest.*

Mark 8:36 *How do you benefit if you gain the whole world but lose your own soul in the process?* No amount of money is worth it if it was gained deceptively or dishonestly. Taking advantage of others to make money is stealing. Those who do this lose far more than they could ever gain.

Philippians 4:11-12 *I have learned how to get along happily whether I have much or little. . . . I have learned the secret of living in every situation.*

Philippians 4:19 *This same God who takes care of [Paul] will supply all your needs from his glorious riches.*
The Bible promises that God will supply all of our needs. The problem comes when our definition of "need" is different from God's. The first thing we must do is study God's Word to discover what he says we need for a fulfilling life.

Mark 12:43 *He called his disciples to him and said, "I assure you, this poor widow has given more than all the others have given."*

170

1 John 3:17 *If one of you has money enough to live well, and sees a brother or sister in need and won't help them—how can God's love be in that person?*

Consistently and generously giving away our money may be the most effective way to keep us from loving it. When we see what giving does in the lives of others, needs are met in us that material possessions can never satisfy. This kind of giving measures our Christian love.

Proverbs 3:9-10 *Honor the LORD with your wealth and with the best part of everything your land produces. Then he will fill your barns with grain.*

Malachi 3:10 *"Bring all the tithes into the storehouse. . . . If you do," says the LORD Almighty, "I will open the windows of heaven for you."*

Luke 6:38 *If you give, you will receive.*

2 Corinthians 9:6 *The one who plants generously will get a generous crop.*

Proverbs 21:20 *Fools spend whatever they get.*

Proverbs 28:19 *Hard workers have plenty of food.*

Matthew 25:14 *He called together his servants and gave them money to invest for him while he was gone.*

1 Corinthians 4:12 *We have worked wearily with our own hands to earn our living.*

1 Thessalonians 4:12 *You will not need to depend on others to meet your financial needs.*
God urges us to be good stewards in earning, spending, and saving our money. He understands the importance of providing for the needs of our family and the future. But he also expects us to use our money generously to help others.

Why do we always seem to want to accumulate more?

Ecclesiastes 10:19 *A party gives laughter, and wine gives happiness, and money gives everything!*
We tend to think money is the answer to every problem.

Mark 10:22 *At this, the man's face fell, and he went sadly away because he had many possessions.*
We accumulate money because we trust money and wealth to bring us happiness. How much more happy and productive we could be if we set our minds to accumulating treasure in heaven.

Why don't I ever seem to have enough?

Isaiah 55:1 *Why spend your money on food that does not give you strength?*
Because we foolishly spend our money on what does not satisfy the soul

Haggai 1:4 *Why are you living in luxurious houses while my house lies in ruins?*
Because we don't manage our money according to God's priorities

Luke 12:15 *Don't be greedy for what you don't have. Real life is not measured by how much we own.*
If we depend on our wealth to bring security, there will never be enough.

Is debt a sin?

Matthew 18:24 *In the process, one of his debtors was brought in who owed him millions of dollars.*
In teaching on forgiveness, Jesus uses this parable that seems to teach that the lending or borrowing of money is not itself sinful, though the manner in which we respond to debt can be.

Proverbs 22:7 *Just as the rich rule the poor, so the borrower is servant to the lender.*
Although borrowing money is not, in itself, sinful, we are to be careful and wise in our borrowing so we don't become slaves to debt.

Proverbs 6:1-3 *If you co-sign a loan for a friend or guarantee the debt of someone you hardly know . . . get out of it if you possibly can!*
Debt is not a sin, but it is a dangerous thing. We are to avoid it whenever possible.

Romans 13:8 *Pay all your debts.*
Although incurring debt may not be sinful, the failure to repay a debt is.

PROMISE FROM GOD: Matthew 6:31-33 *So don't worry about having enough food or drink or clothing. Why be like the pagans who are so deeply concerned about these things? Your heavenly Father already knows all your needs, and he will give you all you need from day to day if you live for him and make the Kingdom of God your primary concern.*

MOTIVES

Does God care about our motives?

Proverbs 20:27 *The LORD's searchlight penetrates the human spirit, exposing every hidden motive.*

1 Samuel 16:7 *The LORD doesn't make decisions the way you do! People judge by outward appearance, but the LORD looks at a person's thoughts and intentions.*
God judges us by our motives.

What are some wrong motives?

James 3:15 *Jealousy and selfishness are not God's kind of wisdom. Such things are earthly, unspiritual, and motivated by the Devil.*

1 John 3:12 *We must not be like Cain, who belonged to the evil one and killed his brother. And why did he kill him? Because Cain had been doing what was evil, and his brother had been doing what was right.*

God is displeased when we are motivated by jealousy.

Genesis 27:11-12 *"But Mother!" Jacob replied. ". . . He'll see that I'm trying to trick him, and then he'll curse me instead of blessing me."*

Fear of getting caught is not a good motive.

1 Samuel 18:17 *Saul thought to himself, "I'll send him out against the Philistines and let them kill him rather than doing it myself."*

It is evil to desire harm for another.

What are some right motives?

2 Kings 2:9 *When they came to the other side, Elijah said to Elisha, "What can I do for you before I am taken away?" And Elisha replied, "Please let me become your rightful successor."*

Wanting to follow in the footsteps of a godly man is a noble motive.

2 Chronicles 1:10 *Give me wisdom and knowledge to rule them properly, for who is able to govern this great nation of yours?*

Solomon's motive, to serve God and rule well and not to serve himself, was very pleasing to God.

John 21:17 *Once more he asked him, "Simon son of John, do you love me?" Peter . . . said, "Lord, you know everything. You know I love you." Jesus said, "Then feed my sheep."*

God wants us to feed his people out of love for Jesus.

PROMISE FROM GOD: Proverbs 14:22 *If you plot evil, you will be lost; but if you plan good, you will be granted unfailing love and faithfulness.*

OBEDIENCE

Since we are saved by faith, why do we need to obey God?

Hebrews 11:8 *It was by faith that Abraham obeyed.*

Obedience is an act of continuous faith.

Philippians 2:12 *Dearest friends, you were always so careful to follow my instructions when I was with you. And now that I am away you must be even more careful to put into action God's saving work in your lives, obeying God with deep reverence and fear.*

Obedience is putting into action God's saving work in our lives.

Titus 1:16 *Such people claim they know God, but they deny him by the way they live. They are despicable and disobedient, worthless for doing anything good.*

If we are disobedient to God, our claim to know him is meaningless.

Leviticus 9:6 *Moses told them, "When you have followed these instructions from the LORD, the glorious presence of the LORD will appear to you."*

Acts 5:32 *We are witnesses of these things and so is the Holy Spirit, who is given by God to those who obey him.*

God's presence in our lives comes when we obey him.

In what ways does God want us to obey him?

Deuteronomy 5:32 *You must obey all the commands of the LORD your God, following his instructions in every detail.*

God wants us to do everything he commands us to do.

Exodus 12:28 *The people of Israel did just as the LORD had commanded through Moses and Aaron.*

Romans 13:1 *Obey the government, for God is the one who put it there. All governments have been placed in power by God.*

Hebrews 13:17 *Obey your spiritual leaders and do what they say.*
God shows us through human authorities what he wants us to do.

Exodus 1:17 *Because the midwives feared God, they refused to obey the king and allowed the boys to live, too.*

Acts 4:19-20 *Peter and John replied, "Do you think God wants us to obey you rather than him? We cannot stop telling about the wonderful things we have seen and heard."*

Acts 5:29 *Peter and the apostles replied, "We must obey God rather than human authority."*
We must obey God over human authorities.

PROMISE FROM GOD: **Psalm 119:2** *Happy are those who obey his decrees and search for him with all their hearts.*

OPPORTUNITIES

How do I prepare for opportunities before they come?

Matthew 9:37-38 *He said to his disciples, "The harvest is so great, but the workers are so few. So pray."*
Pray that God will supply enough people to respond to the opportunities that become available.

Matthew 26:40-41 *"Couldn't you stay awake and watch with me even one hour? Keep alert and pray. Otherwise temptation will overpower you. For though the spirit is willing enough, the body is weak!"* Always be alert and prayerful, in order to respond properly to every situation.

John 12:35 *Jesus replied, "My light will shine out for you just a little while longer. Walk in it while you can, so you will not stumble when the darkness falls."* Walking in Christ's light will help us to be ready for opportunities.

How do I make the most of opportunities that come?

Deuteronomy 1:21, 30 *"Don't be afraid! Don't be discouraged! . . . The LORD your God is going before you. He will fight for you, just as you saw him do in Egypt."* Respond with courage and faith in God when opportunities arise.

Philippians 1:14 *Because of my imprisonment, many of the Christians here have gained confidence and become more bold in telling others about Christ.* Seize opportunities to do good, even when you are experiencing personal hardship.

1 Corinthians 16:8-9 *In the meantime, I will be staying here at Ephesus until the Festival of Pentecost, for there is a wide-open door for a great work here, and many people are responding.*
Be willing to change your plans in order to take advantage of an opportunity.

Acts 11:19 *Meanwhile, the believers who had fled from Jerusalem during the persecution after Stephen's death traveled as far as Phoenicia, Cyprus, and Antioch of Syria. They preached the Good News.*
Use unexpected change or difficulty as an opportunity to serve God.

Acts 21:37 *As Paul was about to be taken inside, he said to the commander, "May I have a word with you?" "Do you know Greek?" the commander asked, surprised.*
Like Paul, we may have to use our wits to take advantage of an opportunity.

PROMISE FROM GOD: Matthew 25:29 *To those who use well what they are given, even more will be given, and they will have an abundance. But from those who are unfaithful, even what little they have will be taken away.*

Revelation 3:8 *"I know all the things you do, and I have opened a door for you that no one can shut."*

OPPOSITION

Why do I sometimes experience opposition or persecution?

2 Timothy 3:12 *Yes, and everyone who wants to live a godly life in Christ Jesus will suffer persecution.*
Living a godly life brings us into conflict with the evil that is in the world.

Matthew 24:9 *"Then you will be arrested, persecuted, and killed. You will be hated all over the world because of your allegiance to me."*
Devotion to Jesus brings opposition and persecution from those who do not want to believe the Good News.

1 Peter 4:15 *If you suffer, however, it must not be for murder, stealing, making trouble, or prying into other people's affairs.*
Sometimes we think we are being persecuted for doing what is right, but in fact we have earned the persecution that we are experiencing.

How should I respond to opposition or persecution?

Psalm 7:1 *I come to you for protection, O LORD my God. Save me from my persecutors—rescue me!*
When we experience opposition or persecution, our first response should be to draw near to God and ask him for his help.

181

Isaiah 53:7 *He was oppressed and treated harshly, yet he never said a word. He was led as a lamb to the slaughter. And as a sheep is silent before the shearers, he did not open his mouth.*
Following Jesus means that we, like him, might have to endure persecution without fighting back.

Matthew 5:44 *But I say, love your enemies! Pray for those who persecute you!*

1 Peter 3:9 *Don't repay evil for evil. Don't retaliate when people say unkind things about you. Instead, pay them back with a blessing. That is what God wants you to do, and he will bless you for it.*
God calls us to answer persecution by loving, blessing, and praying for those who oppose us.

Matthew 10:23 *When you are persecuted in one town, flee to the next.*
Sometimes we might have to flee from persecution.

1 Peter 4:19 *If you are suffering according to God's will, keep on doing what is right, and trust yourself to the God who made you, for he will never fail you.*
No matter how much opposition or persecution we experience, we must continue doing what is right and trusting in God to take care of us.

PROMISE FROM GOD: Matthew 5:10-12 *"God blesses those who are persecuted because they live for God, for the Kingdom of Heaven is theirs. God blesses you when you are mocked and persecuted and lied about because you are my followers. Be happy about it! Be very glad! For a great reward awaits you in heaven."*

PARENTING

What does the Bible say about the role of parents?

2 Timothy 3:15 *You have been taught the holy Scriptures from childhood.*
Parents are to take responsibility for teaching their children a love for the word of God.

Proverbs 3:12 *The LORD corrects those he loves, just as a father corrects a child in whom he delights.*

Hebrews 12:11 *No discipline is enjoyable while it is happening—it is painful! But afterward there will be a quiet harvest of right living.*
Parents are to discipline their children with consistency, wisdom, and love.

Genesis 25:28 *Isaac loved Esau . . . but Rebekah favored Jacob.*
Parents are not to show favoritism between children.

1 Samuel 2:29 *Why do you honor your sons more than me?*
Parents who are too indulgent do not help their children develop character.

Luke 15:20 *Filled with love and compassion, he ran to his son, embraced him, and kissed him.*
The mark of a loving parent is the willingness to forgive.

How are children to relate to parents?

Exodus 20:12 *Honor your father and mother. Then you will live a long, full life in the land the LORD your God will give you.*

Ephesians 6:1 *Children, obey your parents because you belong to the Lord.*
Children have a responsibility to honor and show respect to their parents.

What if I am a single parent or grew up in a single-parent home?

Psalm 68:5 *Father to the fatherless, defender of widows . . .*
God has a special place in his heart for those who are lonely or abandoned.

PROMISE FROM GOD: Proverbs 22:6 *Teach your children to choose the right path, and when they are older, they will remain upon it.*

PATIENCE

How can I grow in patience?

Exodus 5:22 *So Moses went back to the LORD and protested, . . . "Why did you send me?"*
We become impatient when we focus on our own agenda rather than on God's will.

Psalm 40:1 *I waited patiently for the LORD to help me, and he turned to me and heard my cry.*
We must wait patiently for God to do his work in us.

Habakkuk 2:3 *If it seems slow, wait patiently, for it will surely take place. It will not be delayed.*
We develop patience as we learn to live from an eternal perspective.

Galatians 5:22 *When the Holy Spirit controls our lives, he will produce this kind of fruit in us: love, joy, peace, patience.*
Patience is a by-product of the presence and work of the Holy Spirit in our hearts.

1 Corinthians 13:4 *Love is patient and kind.*
Patience is one of the evidences of love.

Romans 8:25 *If we look forward to something we don't have yet, we must wait patiently and confidently.*
Patience is produced by the hope a believer has in God's eternal glory.

PROMISE FROM GOD:
Lamentations 3:25 *The LORD is wonderfully good to those who wait for him and seek him.*

PERSISTENCE

How is persistence an important character quality?

Genesis 18:32 *Finally, Abraham said, "Lord, please do not get angry; I will speak but once more! Suppose only ten are found there?" And the LORD said, "Then, for the sake of the ten, I will not destroy it."*
Persistence in prayer is vital for effective intercession.

Genesis 32:26-29 *The man said, "Let me go, for it is dawn." But Jacob panted, "I will not let you go unless you bless me." "What is your name?" the man asked. He replied, "Jacob." "Your name will no longer be Jacob," the man told him. "It is now Israel, because you have struggled with both God and men and have won." . . . Then he blessed Jacob there.*

Luke 11:8 *I tell you this—though he won't do it as a friend, if you keep knocking long enough, he will get up and give you what you want so his reputation won't be damaged.*

Luke 18:5 *"This woman is driving me crazy. I'm going to see that she gets justice, because she is wearing me out with her constant requests!"*
Persistence is often the key to getting what you want.

Luke 9:62 *Jesus told him, "Anyone who puts a hand to the plow and then looks back is not fit for the Kingdom of God."*

Acts 14:22 *They encouraged them to continue in the faith, reminding them that they must enter into the Kingdom of God through many tribulations.*
Persistence is necessary in our walk with Christ.

How do I develop persistence?

1 Chronicles 16:11 *Search for the LORD and for his strength, and keep on searching.*
We can develop persistence by continuing steadfastly in prayer and seeking the Lord.

Proverbs 4:27 *Don't get sidetracked; keep your feet from following evil.*
Avoiding distractions will help us to develop persistence.

Galatians 6:9 *Don't get tired of doing what is good. Don't get discouraged and give up, for we will reap a harvest of blessing at the appropriate time.*

Philippians 3:13 *No, dear brothers and sisters, I am still not all I should be, but I am focusing all my energies on this one thing: Forgetting the past and looking forward to what lies ahead.*

1 Peter 1:13 *So think clearly and exercise self-control. Look forward to the special blessings that will come to you at the return of Jesus Christ.* Persistence will come if we keep our focus on the task at hand and the promise of blessing to come.

Ephesians 6:18 *Pray at all times and on every occasion in the power of the Holy Spirit. Stay alert and be persistent in your prayers for all Christians everywhere.* Praying and living in the power of the Holy Spirit will help give us persistence.

Hebrews 12:1-2 *Since we are surrounded by such a huge crowd of witnesses to the life of faith, let us strip off every weight that slows us down, especially the sin that so easily hinders our progress. And let us run with endurance the race that God has set before us. We do this by keeping our eyes on Jesus, on whom our faith depends from start to finish.* We must keep our eyes on Jesus and take courage from the example of those who have gone before.

PROMISE FROM GOD: Job 17:9 *The righteous will move onward and forward, and those with pure hearts will become stronger and stronger.*

Matthew 24:13 *Those who endure to the end will be saved.*

PLANNING

Why is it important to plan ahead?

Proverbs 20:4 *If you are too lazy to plow in the right season, you will have no food at the harvest.*

Luke 14:28 *Don't begin until you count the cost. For who would begin construction of a building without first getting estimates and then checking to see if there is enough money to pay the bills?* Planning for the future is necessary to prevent disasters.

Proverbs 13:16 *Wise people think before they act.*

Proverbs 14:8 *The wise look ahead to see what is coming.*

Proverbs 22:3 *A prudent person foresees the danger ahead and takes precautions; the simpleton goes blindly on and suffers the consequences.* Planning and foresight will help us prepare for danger ahead so that we can avoid disastrous consequences.

Doesn't planning ahead conflict with trusting God to lead us?

1 Chronicles 28:12, 19 *David also gave Solomon all the plans he had in mind for the courtyards of the LORD's Temple, the outside rooms, the treasuries of God's Temple, and the rooms for the*

dedicated gifts. . . . *"Every part of this plan,"* David told Solomon, *"was given to me in writing from the hand of the LORD."*

Rather than conflicting with trust in God, planning helps us put our faith in God into action.

Genesis 11:4 *"Let's build a great city with a tower that reaches to the skies—a monument to our greatness! This will bring us together and keep us from scattering all over the world."*

Psalm 33:10 *The LORD shatters the plans of the nations and thwarts all their schemes.*

Making plans without referring to God and his will is a recipe for frustration and disaster.

PROMISE FROM GOD: Proverbs 19:21 *You can make many plans, but the LORD's purpose will prevail.*

PLEASURE

What gives God pleasure?

Job 1:8 *Then the LORD asked Satan, "Have you noticed my servant Job? He is the finest man in all the earth—a man of complete integrity. He fears God and will have nothing to do with evil."*

Matthew 3:17 *A voice from heaven said, "This is my beloved Son, and I am fully pleased with him."*

God takes pleasure in those who are righteous.

John 8:29 *"The one who sent me is with me—he has not deserted me. For I always do those things that are pleasing to him."*
God is pleased when we obey him.

Hebrews 11:6 *So, you see, it is impossible to please God without faith. Anyone who wants to come to him must believe that there is a God and that he rewards those who sincerely seek him.*

Hebrews 11:5 *It was by faith that Enoch was taken up to heaven without dying. . . . But before he was taken up, he was approved as pleasing to God.*
God takes pleasure in those who trust in him.

Ephesians 1:5, 9 *His unchanging plan has always been to adopt us into his own family by bringing us to himself through Jesus Christ. And this gave him great pleasure. . . . God's secret plan has now been revealed to us; it is a plan centered on Christ, designed long ago according to his good pleasure.*
It gives God great pleasure to give eternal life to those who come to him through Christ.

What kinds of pleasure are we free to enjoy?

Ecclesiastes 2:24 *So I decided there is nothing better than to enjoy food and drink and to find satisfaction in work. Then I realized that this pleasure is from the hand of God.*

191

1 Timothy 4:4-5 *Since everything God created is good, we should not reject any of it. We may receive it gladly, with thankful hearts. For we know it is made holy by the word of God and prayer.*
God intends us to enjoy our lives and the good things that he has created for us.

Nehemiah 8:10 *"Go and celebrate with a feast of choice foods and sweet drinks, and share gifts of food with people who have nothing prepared. This is a sacred day before our Lord."*
It is good to enjoy occasions of celebrating God's goodness and love.

John 4:34 *Jesus explained: "My nourishment comes from doing the will of God, who sent me, and from finishing his work."*
The best kind of pleasure is to take delight in doing what God wants.

Psalm 16:5, 11 *LORD, you alone are my inheritance, my cup of blessing. . . . You will show me the way of life, granting me the joy of your presence and the pleasures of living with you forever.*
God wants us to take pleasure in *him.*

What kinds of pleasure are wrong?

Isaiah 5:12 *"Destruction is certain for you who get up early to begin long drinking bouts that last late into the night. You furnish lovely music and wine at your grand parties; the harps, lyres, tambourines, and*

flutes are superb! But you never think about the LORD or notice what he is doing."
It is wrong to pursue pleasure without pursuing God.

Galatians 5:19-21 *When you follow the desires of your sinful nature, your lives will produce these evil results: sexual immorality, impure thoughts, eagerness for lustful pleasure. . . . Let me tell you again, as I have before, that anyone living that sort of life will not inherit the Kingdom of God.*
Pleasure that involves sin leads to eternal destruction.

PROMISE FROM GOD: Psalm 4:7
You have given me greater joy than those who have abundant harvests of grain and wine.

POOR

Doesn't God care that I'm poor? I feel so lonely when I realize how so many others seem to have all they need and I'm struggling.
Isaiah 25:4 *To the poor, O LORD, you are a refuge from the storm . . . a shelter from the rain and the heat.*

Hebrews 13:5 *Stay away from the love of money; be satisfied with what you have. For God has said, "I will never fail you. I will never forsake you."*

Romans 8:35-37 *Does it mean he no longer loves us if we have trouble or calamity, or are persecuted, or are hungry or cold or in danger or threatened with death? . . . No, . . . overwhelming victory is ours through Christ who loved us.*

Does God really care about the poor?

Psalm 35:10 *Who else rescues the weak and helpless from the strong? Who else protects the poor and needy from those who want to rob them?*

Psalm 40:17 *I am poor and needy, but the Lord is thinking about me right now.*

Psalm 72:12 *He will rescue the poor when they cry to him; he will help the oppressed, who have no one to defend them.*

Psalm 102:17 *He will listen to the prayers of the destitute. He will not reject their pleas.*

Psalm 113:6-8 *Far below him are the heavens and the earth. He stoops to look, and he lifts the poor from the dirt and the needy from the garbage dump. He sets them among princes.*

God cares deeply for the poor. And he commands all believers to care for them, too.

What is my responsibility to the poor?

Leviticus 25:39 *If any of your Israelite relatives go bankrupt and sell themselves to you, do not treat them as slaves.*

Proverbs 19:17 *If you help the poor, you are lending to the LORD—and he will repay you!*

Proverbs 22:9 *Blessed are those who are generous, because they feed the poor.*

Isaiah 58:10 *Feed the hungry and help those in trouble. Then your light will shine out from the darkness, and the darkness around you will be as bright as day.*

Matthew 7:12 *Do for others what you would like them to do for you.*

James 2:9 *If you pay special attention to the rich, you are committing a sin.*

God has compassion for the poor, so if we would be godly, we must have compassion for the poor. Compassion that does not reach into our checkbooks or onto our "to do" list is philosophical passion, not godly passion. Helping the poor is not merely an obligation but a privilege that should bring us great joy.

PROMISE FROM GOD:
2 Corinthians 8:9 *You know how full of love and kindness our Lord Jesus Christ was. Though he was very rich, yet for your sakes he became very poor, so that by his poverty he could make you rich.*

POWER

How can I have true spiritual power?

2 Corinthians 3:5 *It is not that we think we can do anything of lasting value by ourselves. Our only power and success come from God.*
Spiritual power comes from God alone.

2 Chronicles 16:9 *The eyes of the LORD search the whole earth in order to strengthen those whose hearts are fully committed to him.*
God gives strength to those who are fully committed to him.

John 15:5 *"Yes, I am the vine; you are the branches. Those who remain in me, and I in them, will produce much fruit. For apart from me you can do nothing."*
Spiritual power comes from living in fellowship with Jesus Christ.

How does God exercise his power?

P s a l m 6 5 : 6 *You formed the mountains by your power and armed yourself with mighty strength.*

J e r e m i a h 1 0 : 1 2 *God made the earth by his power, and he preserves it by his wisdom. He has stretched out the heavens by his understanding.*

H e b r e w s 1 : 3 *The Son . . . sustains the universe by the mighty power of his command.*
God exercises his power in creating and sustaining the universe and everything in it.

P s a l m 1 1 6 : 6 *The LORD protects those of childlike faith; I was facing death, and then he saved me.*
God uses his power to protect those who trust in him.

L u k e 1 2 : 5 *I'll tell you whom to fear. Fear God, who has the power to kill people and then throw them into hell.*
By his power God will carry out his judgment.

R e v e l a t i o n 2 0 : 1 0 *Then the Devil, who betrayed them, was thrown into the lake of fire that burns with sulfur, joining the beast and the false prophet. There they will be tormented day and night forever and ever.*
God by his power has conquered our enemy, the Devil.

M a t t h e w 9 : 6 *"I, the Son of Man, have the authority on earth to forgive sins."*
God uses his power to forgive sins.

John 6:44 *People can't come to me unless the Father who sent me draws them to me, and at the last day I will raise them from the dead.*
God draws people to himself by the power of his Spirit.

John 10:28-30 *"I give them eternal life, and they will never perish. No one will snatch them away from me, for my Father has given them to me, and he is more powerful than anyone else. So no one can take them from me. The Father and I are one."*
By his power Jesus gives eternal life to his followers.

2 Corinthians 12:9 *Each time he said, "My gracious favor is all you need. My power works best in your weakness." So now I am glad to boast about my weaknesses, so that the power of Christ may work through me.*
God exercises his power through our weaknesses.

PROMISE FROM GOD: 1 Peter 1:5 *God, in his mighty power, will protect you until you receive this salvation, because you are trusting him. It will be revealed on the last day for all to see.*

PRAYER

What is prayer?

2 Chronicles 7:14 *If my people who are called by my name will humble themselves and pray and seek my face and turn from their wicked ways, I will hear from heaven.*

Prayer is an act of humble worship in which we seek God with all our heart.

Psalm 38:18 *I confess my sins; I am deeply sorry for what I have done.*

1 John 1:9 *If we confess our sins to him, he is faithful and just to forgive us and to cleanse us from every wrong.*

Prayer often begins with a confession of sin.

1 Samuel 14:36 *The priest said, "Let's ask God first."*

2 Samuel 5:19 *David asked the LORD, "Should I go out to fight the Philistines?"*

Prayer is asking God for guidance and waiting for his direction and leading.

Mark 1:35 *The next morning Jesus awoke long before daybreak and went out alone into the wilderness to pray.*

Prayer is an expression of an intimate relationship with our heavenly Father.

Psalm 9:1-2 *I will thank you, LORD, with all my heart. . . . I will sing praises to your name, O Most High.*
Through prayer we praise our mighty God.

Does the Bible teach a "right way" to pray?

Nehemiah 1:4-11 *For days I mourned, fasted, and prayed to the God of heaven.*
Throughout the Bible effective prayer includes elements of adoration, confession, and intercession, as well as requests.

Matthew 6:9 *Pray like this: . . .*
Jesus taught his disciples that prayer leads to an intimate relationship with the Father that includes a dependency for daily needs, obedience to his word, and asking for forgiveness of sin.

Luke 18:1 *One day Jesus told his disciples a story to illustrate their need for constant prayer and to show them that they must never give up.*
Prayer is to be consistent and persistent.

Nehemiah 2:4 *With a prayer to the God of heaven.*
Prayer can be spontaneous.

Does God always answer prayer?

James 5:16 *Confess your sins to each other and pray for each other so that you may be healed. The earnest prayer of a righteous person has great power and wonderful results.*

1 John 5:14 *We can be confident that he will listen to us whenever we ask him for anything in line with his will.*
We can be confident of God's response to our prayer when we submit first to his will.

2 Corinthians 12:8-9 *Three different times I begged the Lord to take it away. Each time he said, ". . . My power works best in your weakness."*
Sometimes, like Paul, we will find that God answers prayer by giving us not what we ask for but something better.

Exodus 14:15 *The LORD said to Moses, "Why are you crying out to me? Tell the people to get moving!"*
Our prayer must be accompanied by a willingness to obey with our actions.

PROMISE FROM GOD: 1 Peter 3:12 *The eyes of the Lord watch over those who do right, and his ears are open to their prayers.*

PREJUDICE

What does God think of prejudice?

Galatians 2:12-14 *When he first arrived, he ate with the Gentile Christians, who don't bother with circumcision. But afterward, when some Jewish friends of James came, Peter wouldn't eat with the Gentiles anymore because he was afraid of what these legalists*

would say. Then the other Jewish Christians followed Peter's hypocrisy, and even Barnabas was influenced to join them in their hypocrisy. When I saw that they were not following the truth of the Good News, I said to Peter in front of all the others, "Since you, a Jew by birth, have discarded the Jewish laws and are living like a Gentile, why are you trying to make these Gentiles obey the Jewish laws you abandoned?"
Racial prejudice is inconsistent with the good news of Jesus Christ.

John 1:46 *"Nazareth!" exclaimed Nathanael. "Can anything good come from there?" "Just come and see for yourself," Philip said.*
Jesus broke the stereotypes of his time.

John 4:9 *The woman was surprised, for Jews refuse to have anything to do with Samaritans. She said to Jesus, "You are a Jew, and I am a Samaritan woman. Why are you asking me for a drink?"*
Jesus reached across lines of racial prejudice and division.

Acts 10:28 *Peter told them, "You know it is against the Jewish laws for me to come into a Gentile home like this. But God has shown me that I should never think of anyone as impure."*
God wants us to overcome our racial prejudices.

PROMISE FROM GOD: Galatians
3:28 *There is no longer Jew or Gentile, slave or free,*
male or female. For you are all Christians—you are
one in Christ Jesus.

PREPARATION

How should I prepare for the coming of Christ?

Matthew 3:2 *Turn from your sins and turn to*
God, because the Kingdom of Heaven is near.
We prepare for the coming of Christ by turning
away from sin, turning to God in faith, and
purifying our lives by humility and holiness before
God.

Malachi 3:1 *Look! I am sending my messenger,*
and he will prepare the way before me. Then the Lord
you are seeking will suddenly come to his Temple.
We should listen to God's messengers, because their
words will help us prepare for Christ's coming.

Matthew 24:32-33 *Now learn a lesson from the*
fig tree. When its buds become tender and its leaves
begin to sprout, you know without being told that
summer is near. Just so, when you see the events I've
described beginning to happen, you can know his
return is very near, right at the door.
Learn the signs of Christ's coming and watch for them.

Matthew 24:42-44 *So be prepared, because you don't know what day your Lord is coming. Know this: A homeowner who knew exactly when a burglar was coming would stay alert and not permit the house to be broken into. You also must be ready all the time. For the Son of Man will come when least expected.* Because we don't know when Christ will come again, we must be prepared at all times.

Matthew 24:14 *The good news about the Kingdom will be preached throughout the whole world, so that all nations will hear it; and then, finally, the end will come.* When we take part in proclaiming the good news of salvation, we help others prepare for the coming of Christ.

How do I prepare for other important events in my life?

Genesis 14:14-16 *When Abram learned that Lot had been captured, he called together the men born into his household, 318 of them in all. He chased after Kedorlaomer's army. . . . Abram and his allies recovered everything—the goods that had been taken, Abram's nephew Lot with his possessions, and all the women and other captives.* Sometimes we can't prepare in advance for what will happen, so swift action and decision making are necessary.

Ephesians 6:10-11 *A final word: Be strong with the Lord's mighty power. Put on all of God's armor so that you will be able to stand firm against all strategies and tricks of the Devil.*
Prepare for spiritual conflict by "putting on" truth, righteousness, knowledge of the good news of Christ and of God's word, faith, assurance of salvation, and prayer.

1 Corinthians 11:27-28 *So if anyone eats this bread or drinks this cup of the Lord unworthily, that person is guilty of sinning against the body and the blood of the Lord. That is why you should examine yourself before eating the bread and drinking from the cup.*
We should prepare for worship by examining and purifying ourselves.

PROMISE FROM GOD: Matthew 25:34 *Then the King will say to those on the right, "Come, you who are blessed by my Father, inherit the Kingdom prepared for you from the foundation of the world."*

PRESSURE

See STRESS

PRIDE

Why is pride considered one of the "seven deadly sins" when other things seem so much worse?

Ezekiel 28:17 *Your heart was filled with pride because of all your beauty.*
The Bible seems to indicate that pride was the sin that resulted in Lucifer (Satan) being cast out from heaven.

Psalm 10:4 *These wicked people are too proud to seek God. They seem to think that God is dead.*
Pride leads to ignoring God and a life of disobedience.

2 Timothy 3:2-4 *They will be boastful and proud . . . They will be unloving and unforgiving . . . They will betray their friends.*
Pride can destroy relationships faster than almost anything else because it is always taking away from others. Pride strengthens your position at the expense of others. It is selfish.

2 Chronicles 26:16 *When he had become powerful, he also became proud, which led to his downfall.*
An inflated estimation of our past successes leads to prideful behavior and, ultimately, judgment.

Obadiah 1:3 *You are proud because you live in a rock fortress and make your home high in the mountains.*

Pride finds comfort in false security.

1 Corinthians 4:6 *If you pay attention to the Scriptures, you won't brag about one of your leaders at the expense of another.*

Pride can infect our spiritual lives and divide the church.

Acts 12:23 *Instantly, an angel of the Lord struck Herod with a sickness, because he accepted the people's worship instead of giving the glory to God.*

God hates pride and will judge it severely.

When is pride healthy and appropriate?

Romans 15:17 *So it is right for me to be enthusiastic about all Christ Jesus has done through me.*

Paul was proud not of what he had accomplished but of what God had done through him.

Galatians 6:14 *God forbid that I should boast about anything except the cross of our Lord Jesus Christ.*

The only thing we are right to be proud of is what Christ has done in saving us from our sin and from death.

PROMISE FROM GOD: Proverbs 16:18 *Pride goes before destruction, and haughtiness before a fall.*

PRIORITIES

What should be my highest priority?

Mark 12:29-30 *Jesus replied, "The most important commandment is this: 'Hear, O Israel! The Lord our God is the one and only Lord. And you must love the Lord your God with all your heart, all your soul, all your mind, and all your strength.'"*
Our highest priority is to love God.

How can I tell if God is really my first priority?

Deuteronomy 10:12-13 *And now, Israel, what does the LORD your God require of you? He requires you to fear him, to live according to his will, to love and worship him with all your heart and soul, and to obey the LORD's commands and laws that I am giving you today for your own good.*

Exodus 20:3 *Do not worship any other gods besides me.*

Joshua 24:15 *"If you are unwilling to serve the LORD, then choose today whom you will serve. . . . But as for me and my family, we will serve the LORD."*

Luke 12:34 *Wherever your treasure is, there your heart and thoughts will also be.*
If God is the center of your life, you will make your relationship with him your highest priority.

What should be my priority concerning the pursuit of money?

Proverbs 3:9-10 *Honor the LORD with your wealth and with the best part of everything your land produces. Then he will fill your barns with grain, and your vats will overflow with the finest wine.*

Proverbs 23:4 *Don't weary yourself trying to get rich. Why waste your time?*

Proverbs 27:24 *Riches don't last forever, and the crown might not be secure for the next generation.*

1 Timothy 6:9 *People who long to be rich fall into temptation and are trapped by many foolish and harmful desires that plunge them into ruin and destruction.*
Pursue most what lasts longest and strengthens life the best. The Lord will be around forever, long after material things have disappeared! He will give greater joy than riches ever could.

PROMISE FROM GOD: Matthew 6:33 *He will give you all you need from day to day if you live for him and make the Kingdom of God your primary concern.*

PRODUCTIVITY

See EFFECTIVENESS

PROFANITY

They're just words. Why is profanity such a big deal?

Philippians 4:8 *Fix your thoughts on what is true and honorable and right. Think about things that are pure and lovely.*

Our minds are to be filled not with the profane but the holy.

Exodus 20:7 *Do not misuse the name of the* LORD *your God.*

To use the name of God frivolously is to violate God's standard of holiness.

Exodus 21:17 *Anyone who curses father or mother must be put to death.*

To curse one's parents is as serious an offense as doing them physical harm.

Ephesians 5:4 *Obscene stories, foolish talk, and coarse jokes—these are not for you. Instead, let there be thankfulness to God.*

Foul language has no part in a believer's vocabulary.

Titus 2:8 *Let your teaching be so correct that it can't be criticized.*
We are to take care that our speech is pure and cannot be criticized by the unbelieving world.

Psalm 34:12-13 *Do any of you want to live a life that is long and good? Then watch your tongue!*

PURPOSE

How do I find true purpose in life?

Psalm 40:8 *"I take joy in doing your will, my God, for your law is written on my heart."*

Ecclesiastes 12:13 *Here is my final conclusion: Fear God and obey his commands, for this is the duty of every person.*
Meaning in life comes from obeying God and doing his will.

John 17:4 *I brought glory to you here on earth by doing everything you told me to do.*

Romans 11:36 *Everything comes from him; everything exists by his power and is intended for his glory.*
Our purpose in life is to bring glory to God.

Matthew 28:18-20 *Jesus came and told his disciples, "I have been given complete authority in heaven and on earth. Therefore, go and make disciples of all the nations, baptizing them in the name of the Father and the Son and the Holy Spirit. Teach these new disciples to obey all the commands I have given you. And be sure of this: I am with you always, even to the end of the age."*

Part of a Christian's purpose in life includes taking part in fulfilling the great commission and building the Kingdom of God.

Romans 8:29 *God knew his people in advance, and he chose them to become like his Son.*

Part of our purpose in life is to become like Christ and to prepare for eternal glory.

Does God have a special purpose for me?

Acts 20:24 *My life is worth nothing unless I use it for doing the work assigned me by the Lord Jesus—the work of telling others the good news about God's wonderful kindness and love.*

God has given each of us work to do, which is part of his purpose to bring his good news of salvation to all creatures.

2 Timothy 1:9 *It is God who saved us and chose us to live a holy life. He did this not because we deserved it, but because that was his plan long before the world began—to show his love and kindness to us through Christ Jesus.*

Each one of us was chosen by God to live a holy life and show his love and kindness to us through Christ.

PROMISE FROM GOD: Romans 12:2 *Let God transform you into a new person by changing the way you think. Then you will know what God wants you to do, and you will know how good and pleasing and perfect his will really is.*

QUARRELING

See ARGUMENTS

RECONCILIATION

Why is it important to be reconciled to others?

Matthew 5:23-24 *"If you are standing before the altar in the Temple, offering a sacrifice to God, and you suddenly remember that someone has something against you, leave your sacrifice there beside the altar. Go and be reconciled to that person. Then come and offer your sacrifice to God."*

Being reconciled with other people is mandatory to our relationship with God.

Matthew 5:25-26 *"Come to terms quickly with your enemy before it is too late and you are dragged into court, handed over to an officer, and thrown in jail. I assure you that you won't be free again until you have paid the last penny."*
Being reconciled to others is helpful for our own health and self-preservation.

Matthew 18:15 *"If another believer sins against you, go privately and point out the fault. If the other person listens and confesses it, you have won that person back."*
God wants us to resolve our differences with others.

Genesis 33:8 *"What were all the flocks and herds I met as I came?" Esau asked. Jacob replied, "They are gifts, my lord, to ensure your goodwill."*

Proverbs 19:6 *Everyone is the friend of a person who gives gifts!*

Proverbs 21:14 *A . . . gift calms anger.*
Giving gifts can be an important part of being reconciled with other people.

Ephesians 2:14 *Christ himself has made peace between us Jews and you Gentiles by making us all one people. He has broken down the wall of hostility that used to separate us.*
God through Christ has made a way for those at enmity with one another to make peace and be fully reconciled.

How can we be reconciled to God?

Ephesians 2:13 *But now you belong to Christ Jesus. Though you once were far away from God, now you have been brought near to him because of the blood of Christ.*

Colossians 1:20-21 *By him [Christ] God reconciled everything to himself. He made peace with everything in heaven and on earth by means of his blood on the cross. This includes you who were once so far away from God.*

Colossians 2:14 *He canceled the record that contained the charges against us. He took it and destroyed it by nailing it to Christ's cross.*

Through the death of the Lord Jesus Christ, God has made it possible for us to be reconciled to him.

Romans 5:1 *Since we have been made right in God's sight by faith, we have peace with God because of what Jesus Christ our Lord has done for us.*

2 Corinthians 5:20 *We urge you, as though Christ himself were here pleading with you, "Be reconciled to God!"*

We must have faith in what Jesus Christ has done for us in order to be reconciled with God.

PROMISE FROM GOD: Colossians 1:21-22 *You were his enemies, separated from him by your evil thoughts and actions, yet now he has brought you back as his friends. He has done this through his death on the cross in his own human body. As a result, he has brought you into the very presence of God, and you are holy and blameless as you stand before him without a single fault.*

REDEMPTION

See SALVATION

REGRETS

How can I deal with the regrets of my life?

Psalm 51:1-12 *Blot out the stain of my sins. . . . Restore to me again the joy of your salvation.*
Regrets caused by sin are cleansed through heartfelt confession, repentance, and forgiveness.

Ezekiel 6:9-10 *Then at last they will hate themselves for all their wickedness. They will know that I alone am the LORD.*
God sometimes uses brokenness and remorse to bring true repentance.

How can I avoid regrets in the future?

Matthew 27:3 *When Judas, who had betrayed him, realized that Jesus had been condemned to die, he was filled with remorse.*
Judas's self-destructive regrets were caused by a combination of selfishness and a failure to consider the full consequences of his decision.

2 Samuel 12:13 *Then David confessed to Nathan, "I have sinned against the LORD."*
One way to avoid regret is to avoid sin.

PROMISE FROM GOD:
2 Corinthians 7:10 *God can use sorrow in our lives to help us turn away from sin and seek salvation. We will never regret that kind of sorrow. But sorrow without repentance is the kind that results in death.*

REPENTANCE

Why does God want us to repent?

Leviticus 26:40 *"But at last my people will confess their sins and the sins of their ancestors for betraying me and being hostile toward me."*
All of us need to repent because we have betrayed God by our sins.

1 Samuel 7:3 *Samuel said to all the people of Israel, "If you are really serious about wanting to return to the LORD, get rid of your foreign gods. . . . Determine to obey only the LORD; then he will rescue you."*
We must turn away from all other gods in order to worship the one true God.

Proverbs 28:13 *People who cover over their sins will not prosper. But if they confess and forsake them, they will receive mercy.*

Isaiah 55:7 *Let the people turn from their wicked deeds. Let them banish from their minds the very thought of doing wrong! Let them turn to the LORD that he may have mercy on them. Yes, turn to our God, for he will abundantly pardon.*
Repentance is necessary to receive God's mercy.

Ezekiel 18:30-32 *Turn from your sins! Don't let them destroy you! Put all your rebellion behind you, and get for yourselves a new heart and a new spirit. For why should you die . . . ? I don't want you to die, says the Sovereign LORD. Turn back and live!*

Ezekiel 33:11 *As surely as I live, says the Sovereign LORD, I take no pleasure in the death of wicked people. I only want them to turn from their wicked ways so they can live. Turn! Turn from your wickedness . . . Why should you die?*
Repentance is the key to having new life from God.

Matthew 3:2 *Turn from your sins and turn to God, because the Kingdom of Heaven is near.*

Luke 24:47 *"There is forgiveness of sins for all who turn to me."*

Acts 3:19 *Turn from your sins and turn to God, so you can be cleansed of your sins.*
Forgiveness of sins and the Kingdom of Heaven are only for those who have turned away from their sins and turned to God.

Matthew 11:20-23 *Jesus began to denounce the cities where he had done most of his miracles, because they hadn't turned from their sins and turned to God. ". . . You people of Capernaum, will you be exalted to heaven? No, you will be brought down to the place of the dead."*
Refusal to turn away from our sins will bring God's judgment.

PROMISE FROM GOD: Ezekiel 18:21 *"But if wicked people turn away from all their sins and begin to obey my laws and do what is just and right, they will surely live and not die."*

REPUTATION

Should Christians be concerned about their reputation?

2 Corinthians 8:20 *We are anxious that no one should find fault with the way we are handling this generous gift.*
We must take care to build a reputation of integrity so the ministry of the gospel is not hindered.

Matthew 6:1 *Don't do your good deeds publicly, to be admired.*
Jesus warns us not to pursue spirituality in order to impress others.

2 Peter 1:5 *Then your faith will produce a life of moral excellence.*
Any reputation we strive to achieve should result from being fully committed to building spiritual character in our life.

How can a bad reputation be changed?

1 Peter 2:11-12 *They will see your honorable behavior, and they will believe and give honor to God.*
The surest way to influence the way others think of you is by your good behavior.

Deuteronomy 4:6 *If you obey them carefully, you will display your wisdom and intelligence to the surrounding nations.*

Obedience to God brings a reputation for wisdom and intelligence.

Mark 2:16 *They said to his disciples, "Why does he eat with such scum?"*
Jesus doesn't accept us on the basis of our reputation but because his love can transform sinners.

3 John 1:3 *Some of the brothers recently returned and made me very happy by telling me about your faithfulness and that you are living in the truth.*
May we earn the reputation of living according to the standards of the gospel for purity and truth.

PROMISE FROM GOD: 1 Peter 5:6 *Humble yourselves under the mighty power of God, and in his good time he will honor you.*

RESPECT

To whom should I show respect?
Exodus 3:5 *"Do not come any closer," God told him. "Take off your sandals, for you are standing on holy ground."*

1 Samuel 12:24 *Be sure to fear the LORD and sincerely worship him. Think of all the wonderful things he has done for you.*
We must show respect to God above all else.

Exodus 20:12 *Honor your father and mother. Then you will live a long, full life in the land the LORD your God will give you.*
It is very important that we treat our parents with respect.

Exodus 22:28 *Do not blaspheme God or curse anyone who rules over you.*

Ecclesiastes 10:20 *Never make light of the king, even in your thoughts. And don't make fun of a rich man, either. A little bird may tell them what you have said.*
We must respect everyone who rules over us.

1 Thessalonians 5:12-13 *Dear brothers and sisters, honor those who are your leaders in the Lord's work. . . . Think highly of them and give them your wholehearted love because of their work.*
Spiritual leaders must be treated with respect.

Leviticus 19:32 *"Show your fear of God by standing up in the presence of elderly people and showing respect for the aged. I am the LORD."*
Elderly people must be treated with respect.

Ephesians 6:5-9 *Slaves, obey your earthly masters with deep respect and fear. Serve them sincerely as you would serve Christ. . . . And in the same way, you masters must treat your slaves right. Don't threaten them; remember, you both have the same Master in heaven, and he has no favorites.*

Employers and employees should each treat each other with respect.

Romans 12:10 *Love each other with genuine affection, and take delight in honoring each other.*

1 Peter 2:17 *Show respect for everyone. Love your Christian brothers and sisters. Fear God. Show respect for the king.*
We must treat all people with respect.

How do I show respect to God?

Deuteronomy 10:12 *"And now, Israel, what does the LORD your God require of you? He requires you to fear him, to live according to his will, to love and worship him with all your heart and soul."*

Hebrews 12:28-29 *Since we are receiving a Kingdom that cannot be destroyed, let us be thankful and please God by worshiping him with holy fear and awe. For our God is a consuming fire.*
We should show our respect for God by serving and worshiping him with reverence.

Ecclesiastes 5:1 *As you enter the house of God, keep your ears open and your mouth shut!*

Habakkuk 2:20 *The LORD is in his holy Temple. Let all the earth be silent before him.*
Keeping silence in God's presence shows respect for him.

Exodus 20:20 *"Don't be afraid," Moses said, "for God has come in this way to show you his awesome power. From now on, let your fear of him keep you from sinning!"*
Our reverence for God should keep us from sinning.

Leviticus 22:32 *"Do not treat my holy name as common and ordinary. I must be treated as holy by the people of Israel."*
Respect for God means that we show reverence for his name.

Psalm 115:11 *All you who fear the LORD, trust the LORD! He is your helper; he is your shield.*
When we trust in God, we show that we truly respect him.

Acts 10:2 *He was a devout man who feared the God of Israel, as did his entire household. He gave generously to charity.*
Giving to charity is a way to show our reverence for God.

PROMISE FROM GOD: Psalm 25:12-14 *Who are those who fear the LORD? He will show them the path they should choose. They will live in prosperity, and their children will inherit the Promised Land. Friendship with the LORD is reserved for those who fear him. With them he shares the secrets of his covenant.*

RESPONSIBILITY

Why is responsibility an important character trait?

Genesis 39:2-3 *The LORD was with Joseph and blessed him greatly as he served in the home of his Egyptian master. Potiphar noticed this and realized that the LORD was with Joseph, giving him success in everything he did.*

Genesis 41:41 *Pharaoh said to Joseph, "I hereby put you in charge of the entire land of Egypt."*
Responsibility will open doors of opportunity to us.

Jeremiah 31:30 *All people will die for their own sins.*

Ezekiel 18:20 *The one who sins is the one who dies.*

Galatians 6:5 *We are each responsible for our own conduct.*
Responsibility is important because we will each be held accountable for our own actions.

What are some things for which we are responsible?

Genesis 2:15 *The LORD God placed the man in the Garden of Eden to tend and care for it.*

Psalm 8:6 *You put us in charge of everything you made, giving us authority over all things.*
We are responsible for the care of the earth.

225

Genesis 43:8-9 *Judah said to his father, "Send the boy with me. . . . I personally guarantee his safety. If I don't bring him back to you, then let me bear the blame forever."*
We are responsible for keeping our promises.

Exodus 21:19 *If the injured person is later able to walk again, even with a crutch, the assailant will be innocent. Nonetheless, the assailant must pay for time lost because of the injury and must pay for the medical expenses.*
It is our responsibility to compensate others for any injury that we may cause them.

Matthew 12:37 *"The words you say now reflect your fate then; either you will be justified by them or you will be condemned."*
We bear responsibility for the words we speak.

1 Kings 1:6 *His father, King David, had never disciplined him at any time, even by asking, "What are you doing?"*
We are responsible to discipline our children.

John 12:48 *All who reject me and my message will be judged at the day of judgment by the truth I have spoken.*
We will be held responsible for how we have responded to Christ and his message.

PROMISE FROM GOD: Matthew
25:29 *To those who use well what they are given,
even more will be given, and they will have an
abundance. But from those who are unfaithful, even
what little they have will be taken away.*

RESTLESSNESS

I feel restless about my future—is that bad?

1 Samuel 13:12 *I felt obliged to offer the burnt
offering myself before you came.*
When we disregard God's timing in favor of our
own, we sometimes cut corners and displease
God.

Ecclesiastes 1:13; 12:13 *I devoted myself to
search for understanding and to explore by
wisdom. . . . Here is my final conclusion.*
A restless search for truth can lead to a deeper
understanding of God and his purposes.

How do I find peace?

Matthew 11:28 *Jesus said, "Come to me, all of
you who are weary and carry heavy burdens, and I
will give you rest."*
Jesus promises his peace to all who come to him
in trusting faith.

227

Romans 5:1 *We have peace with God because of what Jesus Christ our Lord has done for us.*
Knowing our eternal destiny gives us ultimate peace and security.

Philippians 4:6-7 *Pray about everything. . . . If you do this, you will experience God's peace.*
Being in constant communication with the God of peace gives us real peace.

PROMISE FROM GOD: Isaiah 43:2 *When you go through deep waters and great trouble, I will be with you.*

REVIVAL

How do I know when I need revival?

2 Kings 22:11, 13 *When the king heard what was written in the Book of the Law, he tore his clothes in despair. . . . "We have not been doing what this scroll says we must do."*

Acts 2:37 *Peter's words convicted them deeply, and they said to him and to the other apostles, "Brothers, what should we do?"*
God's word will show you his will and your need to be revived.

Lamentations 3:40 *Let us test and examine our ways.*

Testing and examining our ways in light of God's truth will show us when we need revival.

What can I do to help bring revival?

1 Samuel 7:3 *If you are really serious about wanting to return to the LORD, get rid of your foreign gods. . . . Determine to obey only the LORD.*
Get rid of devotion to all other "gods" and begin serving God only.

Acts 3:19-20 *Turn from your sins and turn to God, so you can be cleansed of your sins. Then wonderful times of refreshment will come from the presence of the Lord, and he will send Jesus your Messiah to you again.*
Humble yourself in prayer, confession, turning away from sin, and turning to God.

Hosea 10:12 *Plant the good seeds of righteousness, and you will harvest a crop of my love. Plow up the hard ground of your hearts, for now is the time to seek the LORD, that he may come and shower righteousness upon you.*

Ephesians 4:22-24 *Throw off your old evil nature and your former way of life, which is rotten through and through, full of lust and deception. Instead, there must be a spiritual renewal of your thoughts and attitudes. You must display a new nature because you are a new person, created in God's likeness—righteous, holy, and true.*

Throw off the old nature of sin and put on the new nature of Christ.

2 Chronicles 15:2, 15 *"The LORD will stay with you as long as you stay with him! Whenever you seek him, you will find him. But if you abandon him, he will abandon you."* . . . *Eagerly they sought after God, and they found him.*
Seek God's presence in your life.

Psalm 51:10 *Create in me a clean heart, O God. Renew a right spirit within me.*

Lamentations 5:21 *Restore us, O LORD, and bring us back to you again! Give us back the joys we once had!*
In prayer, ask God to revive your heart and life.

Joel 2:15 *Blow the trumpet in Jerusalem! Announce a time of fasting; call the people together for a solemn meeting.*
You can invite God's people to come together for prayer, confession, and fasting.

Ezekiel 36:26 *I will give you a new heart with new and right desires, and I will put a new spirit in you. I will take out your stony heart of sin and give you a new, obedient heart.*
God grants revival through his Holy Spirit working in our hearts and lives.

2 Timothy 1:6 *This is why I remind you to fan into flames the spiritual gift God gave you when I laid my hands on you.*
Exercising your spiritual gifts can help revive your life.

PROMISE FROM GOD: Ezekiel 39:28-29 *"Then my people will know that I am the LORD their God. . . . I will leave none of my people behind. And I will never again turn my back on them, for I will pour out my Spirit upon them, says the Sovereign LORD."*

SABBATH

Why did God institute the Sabbath?

Genesis 2:2-3 *On the seventh day, having finished his task, God rested from all his work. And God blessed the seventh day and declared it holy, because it was the day when he rested from his work of creation.*

Exodus 20:11 *In six days the LORD made the heavens, the earth, the sea, and everything in them; then he rested on the seventh day. That is why the LORD blessed the Sabbath day and set it apart as holy.*
God instituted a weekly Sabbath (day of rest) because it reflects his creative work and the blessing that he gave when he had finished Creation.

231

Exodus 23:12 *Work for six days, and rest on the seventh. This will . . . allow the people of your household . . . to be refreshed.*
The weekly Sabbath allowed an opportunity for both people and animals to rest from their work and to be refreshed.

Exodus 31:13 *Tell the people of Israel to keep my Sabbath day, for the Sabbath is a sign of the covenant between me and you forever. It helps you to remember that I am the LORD, who makes you holy.*

Leviticus 23:3 *It is the LORD's Sabbath day of complete rest, a holy day to assemble for worship.*

Deuteronomy 5:14 *"The seventh day is a day of rest dedicated to the LORD your God."*

Isaiah 58:13 *Keep the Sabbath day holy. Don't pursue your own interests on that day, but enjoy the Sabbath and speak of it with delight as the LORD's holy day.*
The weekly Sabbath gave Israel a regular opportunity to remember their covenant with God and to worship him.

Mark 2:27 *He said to them, "The Sabbath was made to benefit people, and not people to benefit the Sabbath."*

Matthew 12:12 *Yes, it is right to do good on the Sabbath.*

The Sabbath was not meant to keep people from doing good.

Are we required to keep the Sabbath today?

Galatians 4:10-11 *You are trying to find favor with God by what you do or don't do on certain days or months or seasons or years. I fear for you.*

Colossians 2:16 *Don't let anyone condemn you for what you eat or drink, or for not celebrating certain holy days or new-moon ceremonies or Sabbaths.*

Clearly we do not become righteous or gain God's approval by observing the Sabbath or celebrating certain holy days.

Christ provides true spiritual rest for our souls through faith in him.

Romans 14:5 *In the same way, some think one day is more holy than another day, while others think every day is alike. Each person should have a personal conviction about this matter.*

There is no hard and fast rule for Christians with regard to the Sabbath.

John 20:19 *That evening, on the first day of the week, the disciples were meeting behind locked doors because they were afraid of the Jewish leaders.*

*Suddenly, Jesus was standing there among them!
"Peace be with you," he said.*

John 20:26 *Eight days later the disciples were
together again, and this time Thomas was with them.
The doors were locked; but suddenly, as before, Jesus was
standing among them. He said, "Peace be with you."*

Acts 20:7 *On the first day of the week, we
gathered to observe the Lord's Supper.*

1 Corinthians 16:2 *On every Lord's Day, each of
you should put aside some amount of money in relation to
what you have earned and save it for this offering.*

Revelation 1:10 *It was the Lord's Day, and I
was worshiping in the Spirit.*
Since the time of the early Christians, the first day
of the week has been the Lord's Day and has
replaced the Jewish Sabbath as a special day of worship.

Matthew 5:17-18 *Don't misunderstand why I
have come. I did not come to abolish the law of Moses
or the writings of the prophets. No, I came to fulfill
them. I assure you, until heaven and earth disappear,
even the smallest detail of God's law will remain until
its purpose is achieved.*
Christ's covenant with us does not abolish the
law but fulfills it. The principle that we all need
weekly rest and an opportunity to worship God
still holds true until heaven and earth disappear.

PROMISE FROM GOD: Hebrews 4:9-10 *There is a special rest still waiting for the people of God. For all who enter into God's rest will find rest from their labors, just as God rested after creating the world.*

SACRIFICE

Why did people sacrifice animals in the Old Testament?

Genesis 3:21 *The LORD God made clothing from animal skins for Adam and his wife.*
When Adam and Eve sinned, God used animals in order to cover their guilt and shame.

Genesis 8:20-21 *Noah built an altar to the LORD and sacrificed on it the animals and birds that had been approved for that purpose. And the LORD was pleased with the sacrifice.*
The first people understood that blood sacrifice was necessary to cover (atone for) sin.

Leviticus 10:17 *The sin offering . . . was given to you for removing the guilt of the community and for making atonement for the people before the LORD.*

Leviticus 17:11 *The life of any creature is in its blood. I have given you the blood so you can make atonement for your sins. It is the blood, representing life, that brings you atonement.*

Hebrews 9:22 *Without the shedding of blood, there is no forgiveness of sins.*
In order for sins to be atoned for and forgiven, death—the shedding of blood—is required. Before Christ, animal sacrifice fulfilled this function.

Exodus 12:3, 23 *Announce to the whole community that on the tenth day of this month each family must choose a lamb or a young goat for a sacrifice. . . . For the LORD will pass through the land and strike down the Egyptians. But when he sees the blood . . . the LORD will pass over your home. He will not permit the Destroyer to enter and strike down your firstborn.*
Animals were used as substitutes for people so that people's blood would not be shed.

Genesis 15:9-10, 17 *The LORD told him, "Bring me a three-year-old heifer, a three-year-old female goat, a three-year-old ram, a turtledove, and a young pigeon." Abram took all these and killed them. He cut each one down the middle and laid the halves side by side. . . . As the sun went down and it became dark, Abram saw a smoking firepot and a flaming torch pass between the halves of the carcasses.*

Psalm 50:5 *Bring my faithful people to me—those who made a covenant with me by giving sacrifices.*
Sacrifice was the way God ratified (sealed) his covenant relationship with his people.

What is the significance of Christ's sacrifice?

John 1:29 *The next day John saw Jesus coming toward him and said, "Look! There is the Lamb of God who takes away the sin of the world!"*

Romans 3:25 *God sent Jesus to take the punishment for our sins and to satisfy God's anger against us. We are made right with God when we believe that Jesus shed his blood, sacrificing his life for us.*

1 Peter 2:24 *He personally carried away our sins in his own body on the cross so we can be dead to sin and live for what is right. You have been healed by his wounds!*

Christ took the punishment that our sins deserved and made atonement for us, not by *covering* our sins, but by *taking them away.*

Matthew 26:26-28 *As they were eating, Jesus took a loaf of bread and asked God's blessing on it. . . . "Take it and eat it, for this is my body." And he took a cup of wine and gave thanks to God for it. He gave it to them and said, "Each of you drink from it, for this is my blood, which seals the covenant between God and his people. It is poured out to forgive the sins of many."*

Christ's death ratifies (seals) a new covenant relationship between God and those who come to him by faith.

Romans 8:3 *The law of Moses could not save us, because of our sinful nature. But God put into effect a different plan to save us. He sent his own Son in a human body like ours, except that ours are sinful. God destroyed sin's control over us by giving his Son as a sacrifice for our sins.*

Animal sacrifices could not take away our sin; only Christ's sacrifice could take away our sin and make it possible for us to have eternal life.

John 3:16 *God so loved the world that he gave his only Son, so that everyone who believes in him will not perish but have eternal life.*

John 14:6 *Jesus told him, "I am the way, the truth, and the life. No one can come to the Father except through me."*

Acts 4:12 *There is salvation in no one else! There is no other name in all of heaven for people to call on to save them.*

1 Timothy 2:5 *There is only one God and one Mediator who can reconcile God and people. He is the man Christ Jesus.*

Because Christ is the means by which forgiveness has been obtained, faith in God through Christ is the only means of salvation.

What kinds of sacrifices does God want us to give him today?

Romans 12:1 *Dear brothers and sisters, I plead with you to give your bodies to God. Let them be a living and holy sacrifice—the kind he will accept. When you think of what he has done for you, is this too much to ask?*

2 Timothy 4:6 *As for me, my life has already been poured out as an offering to God.*
God wants us to give him our whole lives.

Hebrews 13:15 *With Jesus' help, let us continually offer our sacrifice of praise to God by proclaiming the glory of his name.*
When we praise God, we are offering him a pleasing sacrifice.

Ephesians 5:2 *Live a life filled with love for others, following the example of Christ, who loved you and gave himself as a sacrifice to take away your sins. And God was pleased, because that sacrifice was like sweet perfume to him.*

Hebrews 13:16 *Don't forget to do good and to share what you have with those in need, for such sacrifices are very pleasing to God.*
As Christ gave himself for us, he wants us to give ourselves in serving other people—even to the point of giving our lives for them.

PROMISE FROM GOD: Hebrews 9:27-28 *Just as it is destined that each person dies only once and after that comes judgment, so also Christ died only once as a sacrifice to take away the sins of many people. He will come again but not to deal with our sins again. This time he will bring salvation to all those who are eagerly waiting for him.*

SALVATION

What does it mean to be saved?

Romans 4:8 *What joy for those whose sin is no longer counted against them by the Lord.*

Romans 3:24 *Now God in his gracious kindness declares us not guilty.*
Being saved means no longer having our sins count against us but rather being forgiven by the grace of God.

Psalm 103:12 *He has removed our rebellious acts as far away from us as the east is from the west.*
Being saved means that our sins have been completely removed.

Psalm 51:9-10 *Remove the stain of my guilt. Create in me a clean heart, O God.*
Being saved means the stain of guilt has been washed away.

1 Peter 2:10 *Once you received none of God's mercy; now you have received his mercy.*

Romans 3:24 *He has done this through Christ, who has freed us by taking away our sins.*
Being saved means we are forgiven in Christ.

How can I be saved?
Romans 10:13 *Anyone who calls on the name of the Lord will be saved.*
God's word promises salvation to anyone who calls on Jesus' name.

John 3:16 *God so loved the world that he gave his only Son, so that everyone who believes in him will not perish but have eternal life.*

John 5:24 *I assure you, those who listen to my message and believe in God who sent me have eternal life.*
Jesus himself promised that those who believe in him will be saved.

Is salvation available to anyone?
Luke 2:11-12 *The Savior—yes, the Messiah, the Lord—has been born tonight in Bethlehem.*
Jesus was born in humble circumstances among very ordinary people to powerfully demonstrate that salvation is available to anyone who sincerely seeks him.

Revelation 20:12 *The dead were judged according to the things written in the books.*
Salvation is available to all, but a time will come when it will be too late to receive it.

How can I be sure of my salvation?

1 Peter 1:5 *God, in his mighty power, will protect you until you receive this salvation.*
Salvation brings the sure hope of eternal life.

Romans 8:14 *All who are led by the Spirit of God are children of God.*
The Holy Spirit takes up residence in our hearts and assures us we are God's children.

Matthew 14:30-31 *"Save me, Lord!" he shouted. Instantly Jesus reached out his hand and grabbed him.*
We cannot save ourselves from sin, guilt, judgment, and spiritual death. Only Jesus Christ can save us.

Why is salvation so central to Christianity?

Genesis 6:11-13 *The earth had become corrupt in God's sight . . . So God said to Noah, "I have decided to destroy all living creatures."*

Romans 6:23 *The wages of sin is death.*
Salvation is necessary because sin against a holy God separates us from him, bringing judgment and spiritual death.

Exodus 12:23 *When he sees the blood on the top and sides of the doorframe, the LORD will pass over your home. He will not permit the Destroyer to enter and strike down your firstborn.*
Salvation through Christ is dramatically foreshadowed through the Passover lamb.

Acts 4:12 *There is salvation in no one else! There is no other name in all of heaven for people to call on to save them.*
Although it may sound exclusive, the Bible's claim of "one way" to salvation is actually an expression of the grace and kindness of God.

PROMISE FROM GOD: Romans 10:9 *If you confess with your mouth that Jesus is Lord and believe in your heart that God raised him from the dead, you will be saved.*

SATISFACTION

See CONTENTMENT

SEDUCTION

How can we avoid being seduced into doing evil?

Genesis 39:10 *She kept putting pressure on him day after day, but he refused to sleep with her, and he kept out of her way as much as possible.*

If someone is trying to seduce you, stay away from that person as much as possible!

Genesis 39:11-12 *One day, however, no one else was around when he was doing his work inside the house. She came and grabbed him by his shirt, demanding, "Sleep with me!" Joseph tore himself away, but as he did, his shirt came off. She was left holding it as he ran from the house.*

Proverbs 5:7-8 *My sons, listen to me. Never stray from what I am about to say: Run from her! Don't go near the door of her house!*

Run away from temptation as fast as you can!

Proverbs 4:23 *Above all else, guard your heart, for it affects everything you do.*

Don't let yourself become emotionally intimate with a woman other than your wife and family members.

1 John 2:26 *I have written these things to you because you need to be aware of those who want to lead you astray.*

Study God's word in order to keep from being seduced by those who teach falsehood.

PROMISE FROM GOD:
Ecclesiastes 7:26 *I discovered that a seductive woman is more bitter than death. Her passion is a trap, and her soft hands will bind you. Those who please God will escape from her, but sinners will be caught in her snare.*

SELF-CONTROL

What are some steps to exercising self-control?

2 Timothy 2:5 *Follow the Lord's rules for doing his work, just as an athlete either follows the rules or is disqualified and wins no prize.*
Self-control involves first knowing God's guidelines for right living as found in the Bible. Regular, consistent reading of God's Word keeps God's guidelines for right living clearly before us.

Psalm 141:3 *Take control of what I say, O LORD, and keep my lips sealed.*

Matthew 12:36 *I tell you this, that you must give account on judgment day of every idle word you speak.*

James 1:26 *If you claim to be religious but don't control your tongue, you are just fooling yourself, and your religion is worthless.*

245

We exercise self-control by watching what we say. How often we wish we could call back words as soon as they have left our mouth!

Romans 13:14 *Let the Lord Jesus Christ take control of you, and don't think of ways to indulge your evil desires.*

2 Peter 1:6 *Knowing God leads to self-control. Self-control leads to patient endurance, and patient endurance leads to godliness.*
We must ask God to help us with self-control. The better we know God, the easier self-control becomes.

When we need help beyond our own self-control, what should we do?

Psalm 60:12 *With God's help we will do mighty things, for he will trample down our foes.*

Psalm 61:2 *From the ends of the earth, I will cry to you for help, for my heart is overwhelmed. Lead me to the towering rock of safety.*
When we face a problem or temptation too big for us, we should run to God for help.

PROMISE FROM GOD: James 1:12 *God blesses people who patiently endure testing.*

SENSITIVITY

What kind of sensitivity should we try to develop?

Deuteronomy 15:7 *If there are any poor people in your towns when you arrive in the land the LORD your God is giving you, do not be hard-hearted or tightfisted toward them.*

We need to be sensitive and openhearted to the needs of the poor.

Proverbs 27:14 *If you shout a pleasant greeting to your neighbor too early in the morning, it will be counted as a curse!*

We should exercise consideration and sensitivity for others.

Proverbs 28:14 *Blessed are those who have a tender conscience, but the stubborn are headed for serious trouble.*

Above all, we need to be sensitive to sin in our own lives, and discern what is right and wrong.

Acts 13:2-3 *One day as these men were worshiping the Lord and fasting, the Holy Spirit said, "Dedicate Barnabas and Saul for the special work I have for them." So after more fasting and prayer, the men laid their hands on them and sent them on their way.*

247

Acts 16:6-10 *The Holy Spirit had told them not to go into the province of Asia at that time. Then . . . they headed for the province of Bithynia, but again the Spirit of Jesus did not let them go. . . . That night Paul had a vision. He saw a man from Macedonia in northern Greece, pleading with him, "Come over here and help us." . . . We could only conclude that God was calling us to preach the Good News there.*
Christ's followers need to be sensitive to the leading of the Holy Spirit.

How do we develop sensitivity?

Isaiah 6:5 *I said, "My destruction is sealed, for I am a sinful man and a member of a sinful race. Yet I have seen the King, the LORD Almighty!"*
A fresh vision of God's holiness will help us to become more sensitive to the sin in our own lives.

Is God sensitive toward us?

Psalm 89:1 *I will sing of the tender mercies of the LORD forever! Young and old will hear of your faithfulness.*
God is sensitive to our needs, and he has mercy on us.

Matthew 9:36 *He felt great pity for the crowds that came, because their problems were so great and they didn't know where to go for help. They were like sheep without a shepherd.*

Matthew 20:34 *Jesus felt sorry for them and touched their eyes. Instantly they could see! Then they followed him.*

Mark 8:2 *I feel sorry for these people. They have been here with me for three days, and they have nothing left to eat.*

Jesus Christ is sensitive to people's needs.

PROMISE FROM GOD: Ezekiel 11:19 *I will give them singleness of heart and put a new spirit within them. I will take away their hearts of stone and give them tender hearts instead.*

SEX/SEXUALITY

What does God think about sex?

Genesis 1:27-28 *God created people in his own image; God patterned them after himself; male and female he created them. God blessed them and told them, "Multiply and fill the earth and subdue it."*

Genesis 2:24 *This explains why a man leaves his father and mother and is joined to his wife and the two are united into one.*

God made men and women as sexual beings, and the sexual relationship is a key part of husbands and wives becoming one person.

Is sex in marriage only for reproduction, or did God plan for husbands and wives to enjoy it, to delight in one another through sex?

Proverbs 5:18-19 *Rejoice in the wife of your youth. . . . Let her breasts satisfy you always. May you always be captivated by her love.*

Ephesians 5:28, 33 *Husbands ought to love their wives as they love their own bodies. . . . So again I say, each man must love his wife as he loves himself.*
Sex is not for reproduction only but for a bonding of love and enjoyment between husbands and wives. It is an important way for them to experience intimacy.

What rights do husbands and wives have to each other's body?

1 Corinthians 7:3 *The husband should not deprive his wife of sexual intimacy, which is her right as a married woman, nor should the wife deprive her husband.*
Husbands and wives do not completely own their own bodies. When they marry, each mate has a loving claim to the other's body.

Is it so bad if I just think about sex with someone other than my spouse?

Exodus 20:17 *Do not covet your neighbor's house. Do not covet your neighbor's wife.*

Matthew 5:27-28 *The law of Moses says, "Do not commit adultery." But I say, anyone who even looks at a woman with lust in his eye has already committed adultery with her in his heart.*
Lust is adultery in the heart. When you imagine having sex with someone, you have consummated it with that person in your heart.

Will God forgive my past sexual sins? Can I truly start over?

Acts 13:38-39 *In . . . Jesus there is forgiveness for your sins. Everyone who believes in him is freed from all guilt and declared right with God.*
God will forgive any sexual sin if there is true repentance, turning away from that sin, and seeking forgiveness.

Romans 1:24 *God let them go ahead and do whatever shameful things their hearts desired.*
God will not forgive sin when a person persists in that sin. Engaging in persistent, willful sin separates us from God, the only one who can forgive sin.

PROMISE FROM GOD: Hebrews 13:4 *Give honor to marriage, and remain faithful to one another in marriage. God will surely judge people who are immoral and those who commit adultery.*

Song of Songs 7:6 *Oh, how delightful you are, my beloved; how pleasant for utter delight!*

SEXUAL SIN

See ADULTERY, LUST, and SEX/SEXUALITY

SIMPLICITY

What kind of simplicity should we develop in our lives?

Psalm 131:1-3 *LORD, my heart is not proud; my eyes are not haughty. . . . Like a small child is my soul within me. O Israel, put your hope in the LORD—now and always.*

Matthew 11:25 *Jesus prayed this prayer: "O Father, Lord of heaven and earth, thank you for hiding the truth from those who think themselves so wise and clever, and for revealing it to the childlike."* We should have simple, childlike faith in God.

Mark 6:7-9 *He called his twelve disciples together and sent them out two by two, with authority to cast out evil spirits. He told them to take nothing with them except a walking stick—no food, no traveler's bag, no money. He told them to wear sandals but not to take even an extra coat.*

Luke 12:22-23 *Jesus said, "So I tell you, don't worry about everyday life—whether you have enough food to eat or clothes to wear. For life consists of far more than food and clothing."*

Christ calls his followers to material simplicity, out of faith in him.

Acts 2:46 *They worshiped together at the Temple each day, met in homes for the Lord's Supper, and shared their meals with great joy and generosity.*
We should have simple devotion for God and love for one another.

1 Corinthians 2:1 *Dear brothers and sisters, when I first came to you I didn't use lofty words and brilliant ideas to tell you God's message.*
We should keep the message of the Good News simple when we proclaim it.

What kind of simplicity should we avoid?

Proverbs 1:4 *These proverbs will make the simpleminded clever.*

Proverbs 1:22 *"You simpletons!" she cries. "How long will you go on being simpleminded?"*

Proverbs 8:5 *How naive you are! Let me give you common sense.*

Proverbs 14:15 *Only simpletons believe everything they are told! The prudent carefully consider their steps.*

1 Corinthians 14:20 *Dear brothers and sisters, don't be childish in your understanding of these things. Be innocent as babies when it comes to evil, but be mature and wise in understanding matters of this kind.*

We avoid being simpleminded by cultivating wisdom.

PROMISE FROM GOD: Psalm 116:6 *The LORD protects those of childlike faith; I was facing death, and then he saved me.*

Psalm 19:7 *The decrees of the LORD are trustworthy, making wise the simple.*

SIN

Is everyone sinful?

1 Kings 8:46 *"Who has never sinned?"*

Psalm 14:3 *But no, all have turned away from God; all have become corrupt. No one does good, not even one!*

Ecclesiastes 7:20 *There is not a single person in all the earth who is always good and never sins.*

Isaiah 53:6 *All of us have strayed away like sheep. We have left God's paths to follow our own.*

Romans 5:12 *When Adam sinned, sin entered the entire human race. Adam's sin brought death, so death spread to everyone, for everyone sinned.*
All people have sinned against God.

Psalm 51:5 *I was born a sinner—yes, from the moment my mother conceived me.*
We are all born sinful.

Genesis 6:5 *The LORD observed the extent of the people's wickedness, and he saw that all their thoughts were consistently and totally evil.*

Jeremiah 17:9 *The human heart is most deceitful and desperately wicked. Who really knows how bad it is?*
People are wicked in their thoughts and hearts.

Is there a way to be free from sin?

Psalm 51:2-3 *Wash me clean from my guilt. Purify me from my sin. For I recognize my shameful deeds—they haunt me day and night.*

Psalm 139:23-24 *Search me, O God, and know my heart; test me and know my thoughts. Point out anything in me that offends you, and lead me along the path of everlasting life.*

Psalm 19:12 *Cleanse me from these hidden faults.*
Ask God to cleanse your heart from sin.

Isaiah 1:18 *"Come now, let us argue this out,"* says the LORD. *"No matter how deep the stain of your sins, I can remove it. I can make you as clean as freshly fallen snow. Even if you are stained as red as crimson, I can make you as white as wool."*

Zechariah 13:1 *On that day a fountain will be opened . . . a fountain to cleanse them from all their sins and defilement.*

Matthew 26:28 *This is my blood, which seals the covenant between God and his people. It is poured out to forgive the sins of many.*

2 Corinthians 5:21 *God made Christ, who never sinned, to be the offering for our sin, so that we could be made right with God through Christ.*

Hebrews 9:14 *Just think how much more the blood of Christ will purify our hearts from deeds that lead to death so that we can worship the living God.* God has made it possible for the stain of our sin to be removed through the shed blood of the Lord Jesus Christ.

Ezra 10:11 *Confess your sin to the LORD, the God of your ancestors, and do what he demands.*

Isaiah 1:16 *Wash yourselves and be clean! Let me no longer see your evil deeds. Give up your wicked ways.*

1 John 1:9 *If we confess our sins to him, he is faithful and just to forgive us and to cleanse us from every wrong.*

It is necessary for us to confess our sins to God and turn away from them.

Romans 6:6, 18 *Our old sinful selves were crucified with Christ so that sin might lose its power in our lives. We are no longer slaves to sin. . . . Now you are free from sin, your old master, and you have become slaves to your new master, righteousness.*

Galatians 5:24 *Those who belong to Christ Jesus have nailed the passions and desires of their sinful nature to his cross and crucified them there.*

Because of what Christ has done, those who have faith in God are free from the power of sin.

PROMISE FROM GOD: Proverbs 28:13 *People who cover over their sins will not prosper. But if they confess and forsake them, they will receive mercy.*

1 Peter 2:24 *He personally carried away our sins in his own body on the cross so we can be dead to sin and live for what is right. You have been healed by his wounds!*

Status

How important is my status in life?

Genesis 23:4-6 *"Here I am, a stranger in a foreign land, with no place to bury my wife. Please let me have a piece of land for a burial plot." The Hittites replied to Abraham, "Certainly, for you are an honored prince among us. It will be a privilege to have you choose the finest of our tombs so you can bury her there."*

Proverbs 22:1 *Choose a good reputation over great riches, for being held in high esteem is better than having silver or gold.*
Status certainly has its advantages.

Genesis 26:12-16 *That year Isaac's crops were tremendous! He harvested a hundred times more grain than he planted, for the LORD blessed him. He became a rich man, and his wealth only continued to grow. . . . Soon the Philistines became jealous of him, and they filled up all of Isaac's wells with earth. . . . And Abimelech asked Isaac to leave the country. "Go somewhere else," he said, "for you have become too rich and powerful for us."*
Status also has its share of headaches and difficulties.

Matthew 19:30 *Many who seem to be important now will be the least important then, and those who are considered least here will be the greatest then.*
Status in this world matters very little in God's eternal Kingdom.

1 Samuel 2:7 *The LORD makes one poor and another rich; he brings one down and lifts another up.*
Our status, whether high or low, comes from God's hand.

How can I use my status to glorify God?

Genesis 50:20 *As far as I am concerned, God turned into good what you meant for evil. He brought me to the high position I have today so I could save the lives of many people.*
We can use our status to bring blessing to other people.

1 Kings 10:1 *The queen of Sheba heard of Solomon's reputation, which brought honor to the name of the LORD.*
When God's people use their status to build a good reputation, that brings honor to God's name.

2 Kings 23:2 *The king went up to the Temple of the LORD with all the people of Judah and Jerusalem. . . . There the king read to them the entire Book of the Covenant that had been found in the LORD's Temple.*

259

Status and position provide prime opportunities to point people to God.

Mark 10:44 *Whoever wants to be a leader among you must be your servant, and whoever wants to be first must be the slave of all.*

John 13:13-14 *You call me "Teacher" and "Lord," and you are right, because it is true. And since I, the Lord and Teacher, have washed your feet, you ought to wash each other's feet.*

Philippians 2:7 *He made himself nothing; he took the humble position of a slave and appeared in human form.*
Whatever our status, we should serve other people.

PROMISE FROM GOD: Proverbs 3:3-4 *Never let loyalty and kindness get away from you! Wear them like a necklace; write them deep within your heart. Then you will find favor with both God and people, and you will gain a good reputation.*

STEWARDSHIP

Are there any biblical guidelines for how we should use the resources at our disposal?

Leviticus 25:23 *Remember, the land must never be sold on a permanent basis because it really belongs to me. You are only foreigners and tenants living with me.*

Psalm 89:11 *The heavens are yours, and the earth is yours; everything in the world is yours—you created it all.*

Everything belongs to God—whatever we have is held in trust from God.

Genesis 1:26 *God said, "Let us make people in our image, to be like ourselves. They will be masters over all life—the fish in the sea, the birds in the sky, and all the livestock, wild animals, and small animals."*

We have been created to manage God's world for him.

Romans 14:12 *Yes, each of us will have to give a personal account to God.*

God holds each of us responsible for how we manage what has been entrusted to us.

Matthew 24:45-47 *Who is a faithful, sensible servant, to whom the master can give the responsibility of managing his household and feeding his family? If the master returns and finds that the servant has done a good job, there will be a reward. . . . The master will put that servant in charge of all he owns.*

Matthew 25:21 *The master was full of praise. "Well done, my good and faithful servant. You have been faithful in handling this small amount, so now I will give you many more responsibilities. Let's celebrate together!"*

God wants us to use what we are given to serve him faithfully.

Ecclesiastes 11:1-6 *Give generously, for your gifts will return to you later. Divide your gifts among many, for you do not know what risks might lie ahead. . . . Be sure to stay busy and plant a variety of crops, for you never know which will grow—perhaps they all will.*
We should prepare for the future by wisely managing what is entrusted to us.

Deuteronomy 16:17 *All must give as they are able, according to the blessings given to them by the LORD your God.*

Proverbs 3:9-10 *Honor the LORD with your wealth and with the best part of everything your land produces. Then he will fill your barns with grain, and your vats will overflow with the finest wine.*
As we are able, we should give to God's servants and God's work.

Proverbs 3:27-28 *Do not withhold good from those who deserve it when it's in your power to help them. If you can help your neighbor now, don't say, "Come back tomorrow, and then I'll help you."*

Luke 3:11 *John replied, "If you have two coats, give one to the poor. If you have food, share it with those who are hungry."*

Romans 12:13 *When God's children are in need, be the one to help them out. And get into the habit of inviting guests home for dinner or, if they need lodging, for the night.*

We should use our resources to help others who are in need.

1 Corinthians 6:19-20 *Don't you know that your body is the temple of the Holy Spirit, who lives in you and was given to you by God? You do not belong to yourself, for God bought you with a high price. So you must honor God with your body.*

We must also take care of our bodies, because these also belong to God.

PROMISE FROM GOD: Exodus 19:5 *If you will obey me and keep my covenant, you will be my own special treasure from among all the nations of the earth; for all the earth belongs to me.*

Psalm 112:5 *All goes well for those who are generous, who lend freely and conduct their business fairly.*

Strengths and Weaknesses

How can I take full advantage of my strengths and minimize my weaknesses?

Exodus 36:1 *Bezalel, Oholiab, and the other craftsmen whom the LORD has gifted with wisdom, skill, and intelligence will construct and furnish the Tabernacle.*

1 Corinthians 12:7 *A spiritual gift is given to each of us as a means of helping the entire church.* Each of us should use our strengths and skills to build God's "temple," the church.

Ecclesiastes 4:12 *A person standing alone can be attacked and defeated, but two can stand back-to-back and conquer. Three are even better, for a triple-braided cord is not easily broken.* Joining together with others will help us to minimize our weaknesses and maximize our strengths.

Ecclesiastes 10:10 *Since a dull ax requires great strength, sharpen the blade. That's the value of wisdom; it helps you succeed.* God can give us wisdom to know how to more fully develop our strengths.

1 Corinthians 4:7 *What makes you better than anyone else? What do you have that God hasn't given you? And if all you have is from God, why boast as though you have accomplished something on your own?*

We should always remember to give God the full credit for whatever strengths we have.

1 Corinthians 16:13 *Be on guard. Stand true to what you believe. Be courageous. Be strong. And everything you do must be done with love.*

Having faith in God will help us to be stronger.

Jeremiah 20:11 *The LORD stands beside me like a great warrior. Before him they will stumble. They cannot defeat me. They will be shamed and thoroughly humiliated. Their dishonor will never be forgotten.*

2 Corinthians 12:9 *Each time he said, "My gracious favor is all you need. My power works best in your weakness." So now I am glad to boast about my weaknesses, so that the power of Christ may work through me.*

God will stand beside us and help us to be strong, even when we are weak.

PROMISE FROM GOD: Zechariah 4:6 *He said to me, "This is what the LORD says to Zerubbabel: It is not by force nor by strength, but by my Spirit, says the LORD Almighty."*

Ephesians 3:20 *Glory be to God! By his mighty power at work within us, he is able to accomplish infinitely more than we would ever dare to ask or hope.*

STRESS

What causes stress?

Genesis 3:6, 23 *So she ate some of the fruit. She also gave some to her husband . . . Then he ate it, too . . . So the LORD God banished Adam and his wife from the Garden of Eden.*

2 Samuel 11:4; 12:13-14 *David sent for her; and when she came to the palace, he slept with her. . . . Nathan replied, ". . . The LORD has forgiven you, and you won't die for this sin. But . . . your child will die."*

Luke 22:56-62 *Finally she said, "This man was one of Jesus' followers!" Peter denied it. "Woman," he said, "I don't even know the man!". . . At that moment the Lord turned and looked at Peter . . . And Peter left the courtyard, crying bitterly.*

Often stress is of our own doing. When we sin, we bring the stress of painful consequences upon us.

Exodus 16:2-3 *The whole community of Israel spoke bitterly against Moses and Aaron. "Oh, that we were back in Egypt," they moaned.*

Stress comes when we fail to trust God for help.

How can I deal with stress and pressure?

2 Samuel 22:7 *In my distress I cried out to the LORD . . . He heard me from his sanctuary; my cry reached his ears.*

Psalm 55:22 *Give your burdens to the LORD, and he will take care of you. He will not permit the godly to slip and fall.*

Psalm 62:2 *He alone is my rock and my salvation, my fortress where I will never be shaken.*

Psalm 86:7 *I will call to you whenever trouble strikes, and you will answer me.*

Isaiah 41:10 *Don't be afraid, for I am with you. Do not be dismayed, for I am your God. I will strengthen you. I will help you. I will uphold you with my victorious right hand.*

Matthew 11:28 *Come to me, all of you who are weary and carry heavy burdens, and I will give you rest.*

John 14:1 *Don't be troubled. You trust God, now trust in me.*

Hebrews 2:18 *Since he himself has gone through suffering and temptation, he is able to help us when we are being tempted.*

2 Corinthians 4:9 *We are hunted down, but God never abandons us. We get knocked down, but we get up again and keep going.*

Galatians 6:9 *Don't get tired of doing what is good. Don't get discouraged and give up, for we will reap a harvest of blessing at the appropriate time.*

Philippians 2:4 *Don't think only about your own affairs, but be interested in others, too, and what they are doing.*

Our true character is exposed when we are under stress. How do we respond to it so that something good can come from it?

Romans 5:3 *We can rejoice, too, when we run into problems and trials, for we know that they are good for us—they help us learn to endure.*

James 1:2-4 *Dear brothers and sisters, whenever trouble comes your way, let it be an opportunity for joy. For when your faith is tested, your endurance has a chance to grow. So let it grow, for when your endurance is fully developed, you will be strong in character and ready for anything.*

Good character is built from the positive building blocks of life. But it is also built from conquering the stresses and problems of life. What you do with stress not only reveals your character but also helps develop your character.

PROMISE FROM GOD: John 16:33
I have told you all this so that you may have peace in me. Here on earth you will have many trials and sorrows. But take heart, because I have overcome the world.

STUBBORNNESS

What makes people stubborn?

Deuteronomy 1:43 *This is what I told you, but you would not listen. Instead, you again rebelled against the LORD's command and arrogantly went into the hill country to fight.*

Nehemiah 9:16 *Our ancestors were a proud and stubborn lot.*
Stubbornness is rooted in arrogance.

Judges 2:19 *But when the judge died, the people returned to their corrupt ways, behaving worse than those who had lived before them. They followed other gods, worshiping and bowing down to them. And they refused to give up their evil practices and stubborn ways.*
Those who practice evil don't want to give it up, which makes them stubborn against God.

2 Kings 17:14 *They were as stubborn as their ancestors and refused to believe in the LORD their God.*

Refusal to believe in God is a form of spiritual stubbornness.

1 Samuel 8:19 *The people refused to listen to Samuel's warning. "Even so, we still want a king," they said.*

Stubbornness toward God can come from a desire for or a reliance on material security apart from God.

Where does stubbornness lead?

Psalm 81:11-12 *But no, my people wouldn't listen. Israel did not want me around. So I let them follow their blind and stubborn way, living according to their own desires.*

If we persist in stubbornness, God may let us follow our stubborn ways.

Exodus 33:5 *You are an unruly, stubborn people. If I were there among you for even a moment, I would destroy you.*

Psalm 95:8-11 *The LORD says, . . . "They are a people whose hearts turn away from me. They refuse to do what I tell them." So in my anger I made a vow: "They will never enter my place of rest."*

Stubbornness makes us unable to be in God's presence.

Jeremiah 11:8 *But your ancestors did not pay any attention; they would not even listen. Instead, they stubbornly followed their own evil desires. And because they refused to obey, I brought upon them all the curses described in our covenant.*

Those who are stubborn against God will be punished.

2 Samuel 2:21-23 *"Go fight someone else!" Abner warned. "Take on one of the younger men and strip him of his weapons." But Asahel refused and kept right on chasing Abner. Again Abner shouted to him, "Get away from here! I will never be able to face your brother Joab if I have to kill you!" But Asahel would not give up, so Abner thrust the butt end of his spear through Asahel's stomach, and the spear came out through his back. He stumbled to the ground and died there.*

Proverbs 29:1 *Whoever stubbornly refuses to accept criticism will suddenly be broken beyond repair.*

Stubbornness may lead to death or other disaster.

2 Samuel 24:4, 15 *But the king insisted that they take the census, so Joab and his officers went out to count the people of Israel. . . . So the LORD sent a plague upon Israel that morning, and it lasted for three days. Seventy thousand people died throughout the nation.*

If the leaders of a nation are stubborn, it may lead to national disaster.

Hebrews 6:4-6 *It is impossible to restore to repentance those who were once enlightened . . . and who then turn away from God.*
Stubbornness may bring eternal separation from God.

How can I keep from being stubborn?

1 Chronicles 16:11 *Search for the LORD and for his strength, and keep on searching.*
Seek forgiveness and grace from God.

2 Chronicles 30:8 *Do not be stubborn, as they were, but submit yourselves to the LORD.*
Submit to God in worship and obedience.

Hosea 12:6 *So now, come back to your God! Act on the principles of love and justice, and always live in confident dependence on your God.*
Return to a life of trust and dependence toward God.

Colossians 1:21-22 *You were his enemies, separated from him by your evil thoughts and actions, yet now he has brought you back as his friends. He has done this through his death on the cross in his own human body.*
Christ's death provides the solution to our spiritual stubbornness.

Hebrews 3:13 *You must warn each other every day, as long as it is called "today," so that none of you will be deceived by sin and hardened against God.*

Fellowship with other believers, including exhorting and warning one another, can help preserve us from having hard hearts.

PROMISE FROM GOD: Jeremiah 32:40 *I will make an everlasting covenant with them, promising not to stop doing good for them. I will put a desire in their hearts to worship me, and they will never leave me.*

STUMBLING BLOCKS

How can I avoid putting stumbling blocks in other people's paths?

Psalm 69:6 *Don't let those who trust in you stumble because of me, O Sovereign LORD Almighty. Don't let me cause them to be humiliated, O God of Israel.*
Ask God to keep you from causing others to stumble.

Romans 14:1 *Accept Christians who are weak in faith, and don't argue with them about what they think is right or wrong.*
Don't argue about inconsequentials.

Romans 14:21 *Don't eat meat or drink wine or do anything else if it might cause another Christian to stumble.*

1 Corinthians 8:9 *But you must be careful with this freedom of yours. Do not cause a brother or sister with a weaker conscience to stumble.*

2 Corinthians 6:3 *We try to live in such a way that no one will be hindered from finding the Lord by the way we act, and so no one can find fault with our ministry.*
Try to avoid causing offense to others by how you live.

1 John 2:10 *Anyone who loves other Christians is living in the light and does not cause anyone to stumble.*
Loving other people with Christ's love will help you not make them stumble.

Are there stumbling blocks that are unavoidable?

Isaiah 8:14 *He will be a stone that causes people to stumble and a rock that makes them fall.*

Matthew 21:44 *Anyone who stumbles over that stone will be broken to pieces, and it will crush anyone on whom it falls.*

Romans 9:32 *They were trying to get right with God by keeping the law and being good instead of by depending on faith. They stumbled over the great rock in their path.*

1 Peter 2:8 *They stumble because they do not listen to God's word or obey it, and so they meet the fate that has been planned for them.*
The offense of Christ's salvation will inevitably cause some people to stumble.

Luke 17:1 *One day Jesus said to his disciples, "There will always be temptations to sin, but how terrible it will be for the person who does the tempting."*
It is inevitable that some people will stumble and fall into sin.

PROMISE FROM GOD: Psalm 119:165 *Those who love your law have great peace and do not stumble.*

Isaiah 28:16 *This is what the Sovereign LORD says: "Look! I am placing a foundation stone in Jerusalem. It is firm, a tested and precious cornerstone that is safe to build on. Whoever believes need never run away again."*

Success

What is true success in God's eyes?

Acts 16:31 *Believe on the Lord Jesus and you will be saved.*
Faith in Jesus

Matthew 22:37 *Jesus replied, "You must love the Lord your God with all your heart, all your soul, and all your mind."*
Love for God

Psalm 119:115 *I intend to obey the commands of my God.*

1 Kings 2:3-4 *Observe the requirements of the LORD your God and follow all his ways.*
Obedience to God's Word

Matthew 20:26 *Among you it should be quite different. Whoever wants to be a leader among you must be your servant.*
Serving and helping others

Proverbs 16:3 *Commit your work to the LORD, and then your plans will succeed.*
Committing all you do to God and putting God first in your life

Mark 4:19 *All too quickly the message is crowded out by the cares of this life, the lure of wealth, and the desire for nice things.*
True success, that which comes from God, is killed by our attraction to worldly things. When we lust for money, position, power, or fame, we will be tempted to spend our energies to get these things, and that will take us away from a pursuit of God.

Is it OK to try to be successful in this life?

Proverbs 12:24 *Work hard and become a leader; be lazy and become a slave.*

Proverbs 22:29 *Do you see any truly competent workers? They will serve kings rather than ordinary people.*
There are many godly character traits that, if applied to life, often bring material success (hard work, integrity, commitment, serving others, planning).

Genesis 39:2-3 *The LORD was with Joseph and blessed him greatly as he served in the home of his Egyptian master . . . giving him success in everything he did.*

Exodus 33:14 *The LORD replied, "I will personally go with you . . . everything will be fine for you."*
Throughout the Scriptures, there are frequent references to God's blessings for his people. God allows his people to have material blessing but urges them never to sacrifice spiritual matters for worldly wealth.

PROMISE FROM GOD: Psalm 84:11 *The LORD God is our light and protector. He gives us grace and glory. No good thing will the LORD withhold from those who do what is right.*

SUFFERING

Why am I suffering? Doesn't God care about me?

Genesis 37:28 *When the traders came by, his brothers pulled Joseph out of the pit and sold him for twenty pieces of silver.*

Jeremiah 32:18 *You are loving and kind to thousands, though children suffer for their parents' sins.* Sometimes we suffer because of the sins of others and not because of our own sins.

John 9:1-3 *"Teacher," his disciples asked him, "why was this man born blind? Was it a result of his own sins or those of his parents?" "It was not because of his sins or his parents' sins," Jesus answered.* Sometimes the suffering that comes to us is not our fault. It just happens. In this case, how we react to the suffering is the key.

Genesis 3:6, 23 *The fruit looked so fresh and delicious . . . She ate some of the fruit. . . . So the LORD God banished Adam and his wife from the Garden of Eden.*

Leviticus 26:43 *At last the people will receive the due punishment for their sins, for they rejected my regulations and despised my laws.*

Proverbs 3:11-12 *My child, don't ignore it when the LORD disciplines you . . . For the LORD corrects those he loves, just as a father corrects a child in whom he delights.*

Sometimes God sends suffering as punishment for our sins. He disciplines us because he loves us and wants to correct us and restore us to him.

Deuteronomy 8:2 *Remember how the LORD God led you through the wilderness for forty years, humbling you and testing you . . . to find out whether or not you would really obey his commands.*

Sometimes God tests us with suffering to encourage us to obey him.

1 Peter 4:14 *Be happy if you are insulted for being a Christian, for then the glorious Spirit of God will come upon you.*

Sometimes we willingly suffer because we must take a stand for Christ.

James 1:3 *When your faith is tested, your endurance has a chance to grow.*

Sometimes we willingly suffer because it will help us grow and mature.

2 Timothy 3:12 *Yes, and everyone who wants to live a godly life in Christ Jesus will suffer persecution.*

The world hates Christ, so when we identify with him, we can expect the world that inflicted suffering on him to also inflict suffering on us.

Can any good come from suffering?

Job 5:17-18 *Consider the joy of those corrected by God! Do not despise the chastening of the Almighty when you sin. For though he wounds, he also bandages. He strikes, but his hands also heal.* Suffering, or woundedness, can bring great renewal and healing.

Romans 5:3-4 *We can rejoice, too, when we run into problems and trials, for we know that they are good for us—they help us learn to endure. And endurance develops strength of character.*

Hebrews 12:11 *No discipline is enjoyable while it is happening—it is painful! But afterward there will be a quiet harvest of right living for those who are trained in this way.*

James 1:3-4 *When your faith is tested, your endurance has a chance to grow . . . for when your endurance is fully developed, you will be strong in character and ready for anything.*

2 Corinthians 1:5 *You can be sure that the more we suffer for Christ, the more God will shower us with his comfort through Christ.*

2 Corinthians 12:10 *Since I know it is all for Christ's good, I am quite content with my weaknesses and with insults, hardships, persecutions, and calamities. For when I am weak, then I am strong.*

2 Timothy 2:10 *I am willing to endure anything if it will bring salvation and eternal glory in Christ Jesus to those God has chosen.*

When something is for our good, Christ's glory, and the building of his church, we should be happy to accept it, even though it may be suffering.

How do I stay close to God in times of suffering?

Psalm 22:24 *He has not ignored the suffering of the needy. He has not turned and walked away. He has listened to their cries for help.*

Recognize that God has not abandoned us in times of suffering.

Psalm 126:5-6 *Those who plant in tears will harvest with shouts of joy. They weep as they go to plant their seed, but they sing as they return with the harvest.*

Recognize that suffering is not forever. In the dark hours of the night of suffering, it is hard to think of a morning of joy and gladness. But the tears of suffering are like seeds of joy.

Lamentations 3:32-33 *Though he brings grief, he also shows compassion according to the greatness of his unfailing love. For he does not enjoy hurting people or causing them sorrow.*

Recognize that God does not want to see us suffer. A loving God does not enjoy the disciplines of life that must come our way. But his compassionate love and care see us through our times of discipline and suffering.

Matthew 17:12 *Soon the Son of Man will also suffer at their hands.*

Luke 24:26 *Wasn't it clearly predicted by the prophets that the Messiah would have to suffer all these things before entering his time of glory?*

John 3:16 *God so loved the world that he gave his only Son, so that everyone who believes in him will not perish but have eternal life.*
Recognize that Jesus himself suffered for us. Christ suffered the agonies of the cross, which not only embraced incredible physical suffering but also the unthinkable suffering of bearing the sins of the world.

Romans 8:17-18 *Since we are his children, we will share his treasures—for everything God gives to his Son, Christ, is ours too. But if we are to share his glory, we must also share his suffering. Yet what we suffer now is nothing compared to the glory he will give us later.*

Hebrews 2:18 *Since he himself has gone through suffering and temptation, he is able to help us when we are being tempted.*

PROMISE FROM GOD:

2 Corinthians 1:3-4 *All praise to the God and Father of our Lord Jesus Christ. He is the source of every mercy and the God who comforts us. He comforts us in all our troubles so that we can comfort others. When others are troubled, we will be able to give them the same comfort God has given us.*

TEMPER

See ANGER

TEMPTATION

Does temptation ever come from God?

James 1:13 *God is never tempted to do wrong, and he never tempts anyone else either.*

Mark 7:16 *"You are defiled by what you say and do!"*
Temptation originates not in the mind of God but within the heart of man.

James 1:2 *Whenever trouble comes your way, let it be an opportunity for joy.*
Although God does not send temptation, he does delight in helping us grow stronger through it.

What makes temptation so alluring?

Genesis 3:6 *The fruit looked so fresh and delicious . . . So she ate some.*
Satan's favorite strategy is to make that which is sinful appear to be desirable and good.

1 Kings 11:1, 3 *Solomon loved many foreign women. . . . And sure enough, they led his heart away from the LORD.*
Often temptation begins in seemingly harmless pleasure, soon gets out of control, and progresses to full-blown idolatry.

How can I avoid falling into temptation?

Genesis 39:12 *He ran from the house.*
The best strategy is to flee the situation.

Proverbs 1:10 *If sinners entice you, turn your back on them!*
Sometimes our greatest tempters are those whom we think are our friends.

Matthew 6:13 *Don't let us yield to temptation.*
We should make our temptations a constant focus of prayer.

Titus 2:11-12 *We are instructed to turn from godless living and sinful pleasures.*
Christian growth brings an increased awareness and sensitivity to temptation in our lives.

PROMISE FROM GOD:

1 Corinthians 10:13 *Remember that the temptations that come into your life are no different from what others experience. And God is faithful. He will keep the temptation from becoming so strong that you can't stand up against it. When you are tempted, he will show you a way out so that you will not give in to it.*

THOUGHTS

How do I make my thoughts pleasing to God?

Joshua 1:8 *Study this Book of the Law continually. Meditate on it day and night so you may be sure to obey all that is written in it. Only then will you succeed.*

Psalm 119:11 *I have hidden your word in my heart, that I might not sin against you.*

1 Timothy 4:13-15 *Focus on reading the Scriptures to the church, encouraging the believers, and teaching them. Give your complete attention to these matters.*

Study and think about God's word continually, and let his thoughts fill your mind.

1 Chronicles 28:9 *Solomon, my son, get to know the God of your ancestors. Worship and serve him with your whole heart and with a willing mind. For the LORD sees every heart and understands and knows every plan and thought. If you seek him, you will find him. But if you forsake him, he will reject you forever.*

Matthew 22:37 *You must love the Lord your God with all your heart, all your soul, and all your mind.* Serve and worship God with your whole mind.

Matthew 5:28 *But I say, anyone who even looks at a woman with lust in his eye has already committed adultery with her in his heart.*

Mark 7:20-23 *He added, "It is the thought-life that defiles you. For from within, out of a person's heart, come evil thoughts, sexual immorality, theft, murder, adultery, greed, wickedness, deceit, eagerness for lustful pleasure, envy, slander, pride, and foolishness. All these vile things come from within; they are what defile you and make you unacceptable to God."* Get rid of evil thoughts.

Psalm 19:14 *May the words of my mouth and the thoughts of my heart be pleasing to you, O LORD, my rock and my redeemer.*

Psalm 26:2 *Put me on trial, LORD, and cross-examine me. Test my motives and affections.*

Psalm 139:23 *Search me, O God, and know my heart; test me and know my thoughts.*
Ask God to help you have pure thoughts.

Philippians 4:8 *Dear brothers and sisters, let me say one more thing as I close this letter. Fix your thoughts on what is true and honorable and right. Think about things that are pure and lovely and admirable. Think about things that are excellent and worthy of praise.*
Fill your mind with good thoughts.

Colossians 3:2-3 *Let heaven fill your thoughts. Do not think only about things down here on earth. For you died when Christ died, and your real life is hidden with Christ in God.*
Think about heaven.

Romans 12:2 *Let God transform you into a new person by changing the way you think. Then you will know what God wants you to do, and you will know how good and pleasing and perfect his will really is.*
Let God change your thoughts.

PROMISE FROM GOD:
1 Chronicles 29:17 *I know, my God, that you examine our hearts and rejoice when you find integrity there.*

TITHING

Why did God require tithes from Israel in the Old Testament?

Leviticus 27:30 *"A tenth of the produce of the land, whether grain or fruit, belongs to the LORD and must be set apart to him as holy."*

Numbers 18:20-24 *The LORD said to Aaron, "You priests will receive no inheritance of land or share of property among the people of Israel. I am your inheritance and your share. . . . The Levites will receive no inheritance of land among the Israelites, because I have given them the Israelites' tithes, which have been set apart as offerings to the LORD. This will be the Levites' share."*

The tithes were necessary to support the priesthood— the ordained spiritual leaders who were responsible for Israel's worship and spiritual life.

Deuteronomy 14:22-27 *You must set aside a tithe of your crops—one-tenth of all the crops you harvest each year. . . . The purpose of tithing is to teach you always to fear the LORD your God.*

Giving one-tenth of their income to God taught Israel to reverence him and recognize their dependence on him.

Are we required to tithe to God today?

1 Timothy 5:17-18 *Elders who do their work well should be paid well, especially those who work hard at both preaching and teaching. For the Scripture says, "Do not keep an ox from eating as it treads out the grain." And in another place, "Those who work deserve their pay!"*

The need to support the spiritual leaders of the church financially has not changed from the Old to the New Testament.

Philippians 4:18-19 *I am generously supplied with the gifts you sent me with Epaphroditus. . . . And this same God who takes care of me will supply all your needs from his glorious riches, which have been given to us in Christ Jesus.*

Giving to God can help us to learn, like Israel in the Old Testament, to reverence God and realize how much he is taking care of us.

Proverbs 3:9 *Honor the LORD with your wealth and with the best part of everything your land produces.*

Giving the firstfruits of our wealth and income to God honors him.

Matthew 5:42 *Give to those who ask, and don't turn away from those who want to borrow.*

Romans 12:8 *If you have money, share it generously.*

Christ calls us to give freely and share with others.

2 Corinthians 9:7 *You must each make up your own mind as to how much you should give. Don't give reluctantly or in response to pressure. For God loves the person who gives cheerfully.*
Each of us is responsible to decide how much we should give. Whatever it is, we should give it cheerfully.

Matthew 23:23 *You should tithe.*
Jesus affirmed the need to give tithes to God.

Proverbs 21:13 *Those who shut their ears to the cries of the poor will be ignored in their own time of need.*

1 Corinthians 16:1-2 *Now about the money being collected for the Christians in Jerusalem: . . . On every Lord's Day, each of you should put aside some amount of money in relation to what you have earned and save it for this offering.*
God wants us to give in order to take care of the poor.

PROMISE FROM GOD: Malachi 3:10 *"Bring all the tithes into the storehouse so there will be enough food in my Temple. If you do," says the LORD Almighty, "I will open the windows of heaven for you. I will pour out a blessing so great you won't have enough room to take it in! Try it! Let me prove it to you!"*

Luke 6:38 *If you give, you will receive. Your gift will return to you in full measure, pressed down, shaken together to make room for more, and running over. Whatever measure you use in giving—large or small—it will be used to measure what is given back to you.*

VALUES

How do I cultivate godly values?

Genesis 39:8-9 *Joseph refused. "Look," he told her, "my master trusts me with everything in his entire household . . . How could I ever do such a wicked thing? It would be a great sin against God."* Refuse to give in to what the Bible says is wrong.

Matthew 7:12 *Do for others what you would like them to do for you. This is a summary of all that is taught in the law.*

Galatians 5:22-23 *When the Holy Spirit controls our lives, he will produce this kind of fruit in us: love, joy, peace, patience, kindness, goodness, faithfulness, gentleness, and self-control.* Godly living is the fruit of God living in us. Godly living is recognized as good, moral living by those around us, but we know it is merely the fruit of God the Holy Spirit living within us.

Psalm 15:1-2 *Who may worship in your sanctuary, LORD? . . . Those who lead blameless lives and do what is right, speaking the truth from sincere hearts.*

Micah 6:8 *The LORD has already told you what is good, and this is what he requires: to do what is right, to love mercy, and to walk humbly with your God.*

How do I take inventory of my current values?

Romans 1:29 *Their lives became full of every kind of wickedness, sin, greed, hate, envy, murder, fighting, deception, malicious behavior, and gossip.*

Ephesians 5:4 *Obscene stories, foolish talk, and coarse jokes—these are not for you. Instead, let there be thankfulness to God.*

Proverbs 30:8 *First, help me never to tell a lie.* How do you view acts the Bible calls sins, such as gossip, flattery, profanity, lying, or cheating? If you don't see these as sins, you must face up to the fact that your values differ from the Bible's.

Matthew 15:19 *From the heart come evil thoughts, murder, adultery, all other sexual immorality, theft, lying and slander.* The heart is the wellspring of moral, or immoral, behavior. Conduct is the fruit of character, and character is the fruit of belief.

How important is it for us to live consistent moral lives?

P s a l m 2 4 : 3 - 4 *Who may climb the mountain of the LORD? Who may stand in his holy place? Only those whose hands and hearts are pure.*

P r o v e r b s 2 8 : 2 *When there is moral rot within a nation, its government topples easily.*

E x o d u s 2 3 : 2 4 *Do not worship the gods of these other nations or serve them in any way.*

PROMISE FROM GOD: R o m a n s 5 : 3 - 5 *We can rejoice, too, when we run into problems and trials, for we know that they are good for us—they help us learn to endure. And endurance develops strength of character in us, and character strengthens our confident expectation of salvation. And this expectation will not disappoint us. For we know how dearly God loves us, because he has given us the Holy Spirit to fill our hearts with his love.*

VISION

Why is having vision important?

2 K i n g s 6 : 1 7 *Elisha prayed, "O LORD, open his eyes and let him see!" The LORD opened his servant's eyes, and when he looked up, he saw that the hillside around Elisha was filled with horses and chariots of fire.*

Spiritual vision can help us see God's strength and be encouraged.

Daniel 4:34 *After this time had passed, I, Nebuchadnezzar, looked up to heaven. My sanity returned, and I praised and worshiped the Most High and honored the one who lives forever. His rule is everlasting, and his kingdom is eternal.*

When we have vision, we see everything in proper perspective.

Isaiah 6:10 *Harden the hearts of these people. Close their ears, and shut their eyes. That way, they will not see with their eyes, hear with their ears, understand with their hearts, and turn to me for healing.*

To receive God's blessings, it is necessary to have spiritual vision.

Matthew 14:29-30 *"All right, come," Jesus said. So Peter went over the side of the boat and walked on the water toward Jesus. But when he looked around at the high waves, he was terrified and began to sink. "Save me, Lord!" he shouted.*

Hebrews 11:27 *It was by faith that Moses left the land of Egypt. He was not afraid of the king. Moses kept right on going because he kept his eyes on the one who is invisible.*

Having a strong vision of Christ will sustain us in crisis.

How do I obtain good spiritual vision?

Psalm 17:15 *Because I have done what is right, I will see you. When I awake, I will be fully satisfied, for I will see you face to face.*

Matthew 5:8 *God blesses those whose hearts are pure, for they will see God.*
Purity of heart and life will enable us to have strong spiritual vision.

2 Corinthians 3:14 *But the people's minds were hardened, and even to this day whenever the old covenant is being read, a veil covers their minds so they cannot understand the truth. And this veil can be removed only by believing in Christ.*
We gain spiritual vision by believing in Christ.

PROMISE FROM GOD: Psalm 34:5 *Those who look to him for help will be radiant with joy; no shadow of shame will darken their faces.*

1 Corinthians 13:12 *Now we see things imperfectly as in a poor mirror, but then we will see everything with perfect clarity.*

Revelation 22:4 *They will see his face.*

VOWS

See FAITHFULNESS and WORDS

VULNERABILITY

Are there ways in which I should be vulnerable?

Genesis 2:25 *Although Adam and his wife were both naked, neither of them felt any shame.*
We should be vulnerable to our wives.

Psalm 139:23-24 *Search me, O God, and know my heart; test me and know my thoughts. Point out anything in me that offends you, and lead me along the path of everlasting life.*

Hebrews 4:12-13 *The word of God is full of living power. It is sharper than the sharpest knife, cutting deep into our innermost thoughts and desires. It exposes us for what we really are. Nothing in all creation can hide from him. Everything is naked and exposed before his eyes. This is the God to whom we must explain all that we have done.*
We should open our hearts and lives fully to God and let him do his work in us.

2 Corinthians 11:27 *I have lived with weariness and pain and sleepless nights. Often I have been hungry and thirsty and have gone without food. Often I have shivered with cold, without enough clothing to keep me warm.*
We should be willing to accept difficulty and danger in order to serve God.

Hebrews 10:33 *Sometimes you were exposed to public ridicule and were beaten, and sometimes you helped others who were suffering the same things.*

Matthew 5:11-12 *"God blesses you when you are mocked and persecuted and lied about because you are my followers. Be happy about it! Be very glad! For a great reward awaits you in heaven. And remember, the ancient prophets were persecuted, too."* We should be willing to suffer humiliation and shame for Christ.

How should I treat those who are vulnerable?

Genesis 9:22-23 *Ham, the father of Canaan, saw that his father was naked and went outside and told his brothers. Shem and Japheth took a robe, held it over their shoulders, walked backward into the tent, and covered their father's naked body. As they did this, they looked the other way so they wouldn't see him naked.*

Proverbs 23:10 *Don't steal the land of defenseless orphans by moving the ancient boundary markers.*
We should do what we can to "cover" those who are vulnerable, and we should not take advantage of their innocence.

Job 6:16 *One should be kind to a fainting friend.*

Isaiah 58:7 *I want you to share your food with the hungry and to welcome poor wanderers into your homes. Give clothes to those who need them, and do not hide from relatives who need your help.*
We should help those who are vulnerable and treat them with mercy, compassion, and kindness.

Psalm 82:4 *Rescue the poor and helpless; deliver them from the grasp of evil people.*

Proverbs 31:9 *Yes, speak up for the poor and helpless, and see that they get justice.*
God wants us to rescue the vulnerable so others will not take advantage of them.

PROMISE FROM GOD: Psalm 12:5 *The LORD replies, "I have seen violence done to the helpless, and I have heard the groans of the poor. Now I will rise up to rescue them, as they have longed for me to do."*

Proverbs 5:21 *The LORD sees clearly what a man does, examining every path he takes.*

Ecclesiastes 5:15 *People who live only for wealth come to the end of their lives as naked and empty-handed as on the day they were born.*

WILL OF GOD

See GOD'S WILL

WISDOM

What are the benefits of having wisdom?

Ecclesiastes 10:10 *Since a dull ax requires great strength, sharpen the blade. That's the value of wisdom; it helps you succeed.*

Wisdom will help you to succeed in what you do.

Ephesians 5:15-17 *Be careful how you live, not as fools but as those who are wise.*

Wisdom helps you know how to live.

1 Kings 3:9-10 *Give me an understanding mind so that I can govern your people well and know the difference between right and wrong.*

The more responsibility you have, the more of God's wisdom you need in order to do what is right.

Proverbs 3:21-26 *My child, don't lose sight of good planning and insight. Hang on to them, for they fill you with life and bring you honor and respect. They keep you safe on your way and keep your feet from stumbling. You can lie down without fear and enjoy pleasant dreams. You need not be afraid of disaster or the destruction that comes upon the wicked, for the LORD is your security. He will keep your foot from being caught in a trap.*

Wisdom will help preserve you from trouble and disaster.

Proverbs 9:11-12 *Wisdom will multiply your days and add years to your life. If you become wise, you will be the one to benefit. If you scorn wisdom, you will be the one to suffer.*
Wisdom will give you a richer, fuller life.

How do I obtain wisdom?

Job 28:12, 21 *But do people know where to find wisdom? Where can they find understanding? No one knows where to find it, for it is not found among the living. . . . For it is hidden from the eyes of all humanity.*
Wisdom is not easy for people to obtain.

Job 28:23-24, 27 *"God surely knows where it can be found, for he . . . established it and examined it thoroughly."*
God holds all wisdom in his hands.

Proverbs 9:10 *Fear of the LORD is the beginning of wisdom. Knowledge of the Holy One results in understanding.*
Wisdom comes from having a relationship with God.

Deuteronomy 4:5-6 *You must obey these laws and regulations. . . . If you obey them carefully, you will display your wisdom and intelligence to the surrounding nations. When they hear about these laws, they will exclaim, "What other nation is as wise and prudent as this!"*

Obedience to God's word—his commands, laws, and teachings—will make us wise.

Psalm 5:8 *Lead me in the right path, O LORD. . . . Tell me clearly what to do, and show me which way to turn.*

James 1:5 *If you need wisdom—if you want to know what God wants you to do—ask him, and he will gladly tell you. He will not resent your asking.* If you need wisdom, ask God, and he will give it.

Colossians 3:16 *Let the words of Christ, in all their richness, live in your hearts and make you wise. Use his words to teach and counsel each other.* Listening to Christ's teachings and obeying his words will give wisdom.

Psalm 25:8-9 *The LORD . . . leads the humble in what is right, teaching them his way.*

Proverbs 3:7 *Don't be impressed with your own wisdom. Instead, fear the LORD and turn your back on evil.* God gives wisdom and guidance to those who are humble.

Proverbs 8:12, 17 *"I, Wisdom, live together with good judgment. I know where to discover knowledge and discernment. . . . I love all who love me. Those who search for me will surely find me."* Those who seek wisdom are the ones who will find it.

Proverbs 20:18 *Plans succeed through good counsel; don't go to war without the advice of others.* Wisdom can be found in the counsel of people who have wisdom.

PROMISE FROM GOD: Proverbs 3:35 *The wise inherit honor, but fools are put to shame!*

Proverbs 24:5 *A wise man is mightier than a strong man, and a man of knowledge is more powerful than a strong man.*

WITNESSING

Is witnessing really necessary?

Psalm 107:2 *Has the LORD redeemed you? Then speak out! Tell others he has saved you from your enemies.*

Mark 16:15 *He told them, "Go into all the world and preach the Good News to everyone, everywhere."* God commands us to tell others about what he has done.

Mark 1:17 *Jesus called out to them, "Come, be my disciples, and I will show you how to fish for people!"*

Acts 10:42 *He ordered us to preach everywhere and to testify that Jesus is ordained of God to be the judge of all—the living and the dead.*

Evangelism is an intrinsic part of being Christ's followers.

2 Kings 7:9 *"This is not right. This is wonderful news, and we aren't sharing it with anyone! . . . Come on, let's go back and tell the people."*
It is not right for us to keep the Good News to ourselves. Our witness is the only way some people will ever hear the Good News.

Romans 10:14 *But how can they call on him to save them unless they believe in him? And how can they believe in him if they have never heard about him? And how can they hear about him unless someone tells them? And how will anyone go and tell them without being sent?*
The only way that people can be saved is by hearing and believing the message of Good News that we have.

Ezekiel 3:18 *If I warn the wicked, saying, "You are under the penalty of death," but you fail to deliver the warning, they will die in their sins. And I will hold you responsible, demanding your blood for theirs.*
If we are silent about Christ, we will be subject to punishment.

Jude 1:23 *Rescue others by snatching them from the flames of judgment. There are still others to whom you need to show mercy, but be careful that you aren't contaminated by their sins.*
We must rescue others from the flames of judgment.

What should my witnessing include?

Exodus 18:9 *Moses told his father-in-law about everything the LORD had done to rescue Israel.*

John 9:25 *"I don't know whether he is a sinner," the man replied. "But I know this: I was blind, and now I can see!"*
Your witness should include telling others how God has rescued you and healed your sin-blinded heart.

Psalm 28:6 *Praise the LORD! For he has heard my cry for mercy.*
Proclaim how God has answered your prayers.

Psalm 30:3 *You brought me up from the grave, O LORD. You kept me from falling into the pit of death.*
Explain how God has saved you from spiritual death.

Acts 4:33 *The apostles gave powerful witness to the resurrection of the Lord Jesus, and God's great favor was upon them all.*
Be sure to tell others the news of Christ's resurrection.

Acts 10:42 *He ordered us to preach everywhere and to testify that Jesus is ordained of God to be the judge of all—the living and the dead.*
Warn people about the coming judgment by the living Christ.

1 Peter 3:15 *If you are asked about your Christian hope, always be ready to explain it.*
Be ready to explain why you have hope.

1 John 1:2 *We testify and announce to you that he is the one who is eternal life.*
Tell others the good news that eternal life is found in Christ.

1 Corinthians 2:2 *I decided to concentrate only on Jesus Christ and his death on the cross.*
Tell how Jesus died on the cross to take away our sins.

Luke 24:47 *With my authority, take this message of repentance to all the nations, beginning in Jerusalem: "There is forgiveness of sins for all who turn to me."*
Explain the message of repentance, forgiveness, and reconciliation with God.

Romans 10:9 *If you confess with your mouth that Jesus is Lord and believe in your heart that God raised him from the dead, you will be saved.*
Make clear the need to confess Christ as Lord and believe in his resurrection.

1 Thessalonians 1:5 *You know that the way we lived among you was further proof of the truth of our message.*
How you live is an important element of your witness for Christ.

PROMISE FROM GOD: Daniel 12:3
Those who are wise will shine as bright as the sky, and those who turn many to righteousness will shine like stars forever.

WIVES

How does God want men to treat their wives?

Proverbs 18:22 *The man who finds a wife finds a treasure and receives favor from the LORD.*
We should treat our wives as the treasures that they really are.

Genesis 2:23 *"At last!" Adam exclaimed. "She is part of my own flesh and bone! She will be called 'woman,' because she was taken out of a man."*
We should always maintain an appreciative attitude toward our wife.

1 Corinthians 7:3-5 *The husband should not deprive his wife of sexual intimacy, which is her right as a married woman, nor should the wife deprive her husband. . . . So do not deprive each other of sexual relations.*
We should give our wives sexual intimacy and not withhold it.

1 Corinthians 7:32-34 *An unmarried man can spend his time doing the Lord's work and thinking how to please him. But a married man can't do that so well. He has to think about his earthly responsibilities and how to please his wife.*

We must forego some of our own plans or ministries in order to take care of our wives and please them.

Ephesians 5:23 *A husband is the head of his wife as Christ is the head of his body, the church; he gave his life to be her Savior.*

In the marriage relationship we need to exercise responsibility and leadership, which involves giving our life for our wife.

Ephesians 5:25-33 *You husbands must love your wives with the same love Christ showed the church. . . . Husbands ought to love their wives as they love their own bodies. . . . No one hates his own body but lovingly cares for it. . . . Each man must love his wife as he loves himself.*

Colossians 3:19 *You husbands must love your wives and never treat them harshly.*

We must love our wives with sacrificial love and treat them with gentleness and kindness.

1 Peter 3:7 *In the same way, you husbands must give honor to your wives. Treat her with understanding as you live together. She may be weaker than you are, but she is your equal partner in God's gift of new life.*

We must treat our wives with honor and understanding.

What should men expect from their wives?

Judges 13:22-23 *He said to his wife, "We will die, for we have seen God!" But his wife said, "If the LORD were going to kill us, he . . . wouldn't have appeared to us and told us this wonderful thing and done these miracles."*

Matthew 27:19 *As Pilate was sitting on the judgment seat, his wife sent him this message: "Leave that innocent man alone, because I had a terrible nightmare about him last night."*
We should expect that our wives will sometimes have wisdom and spiritual insight that we don't have ourselves.

Job 2:9-10 *His wife said to him, "Are you still trying to maintain your integrity? Curse God and die." But Job replied, ". . . Should we accept only good things from the hand of God and never anything bad?"*
We should also expect that we will sometimes have wisdom and spiritual insight that our wives don't have.

Matthew 1:18-19 *This is how Jesus the Messiah was born. His mother, Mary, was engaged to be married to Joseph. But while she was still a virgin, she became pregnant by the Holy Spirit. Joseph, her fiancé, being a just man, decided to break the engagement quietly, so as not to disgrace her publicly.*
We should expect that our wives will be faithful to us in marriage.

2 Chronicles 21:6 *Jehoram followed the example of the kings of Israel and was as wicked as King Ahab, for he had married one of Ahab's daughters. So Jehoram did what was evil in the LORD's sight.*
We should expect our wives to influence our decisions, either for good or for evil.

PROMISE FROM GOD: Psalm 128:3-4 *Your wife will be like a fruitful vine, flourishing within your home. . . . That is the LORD's reward for those who fear him.*

1 Peter 3:7 *If you don't treat her as you should, your prayers will not be heard.*

WORDS

Do my words really matter?

Deuteronomy 23:23 *But once you have voluntarily made a vow, be careful to do as you have said, for you have made a vow to the LORD your God.*

Joshua 9:18-20 *The leaders replied, "We have sworn an oath in the presence of the LORD, the God of Israel. We cannot touch them. We must let them live, for God would be angry with us if we broke our oath."*

When we say we will do something, it is a binding commitment.

Psalm 15:1-3 *Who may worship in your sanctuary, LORD? Who may enter your presence on your holy hill? Those who lead blameless lives and do what is right, speaking the truth from sincere hearts. Those who refuse to slander others or harm their neighbors or speak evil of their friends.*

Our words matter to God; only those who speak rightly can enter his presence.

James 1:26 *If you claim to be religious but don't control your tongue, you are just fooling yourself, and your religion is worthless.*

Our words show what kind of people we really are.

Proverbs 11:11 *Upright citizens bless a city and make it prosper, but the talk of the wicked tears it apart.*

Proverbs 15:1 *A gentle answer turns away wrath, but harsh words stir up anger.*
Words of blessing and wicked words are both very powerful.

Proverbs 17:9 *Disregarding another person's faults preserves love; telling about them separates close friends.*
What we say makes a real difference in our relationships.

Matthew 12:36-37 *I tell you this, that you must give an account on judgment day of every idle word you speak. The words you say now reflect your fate then; either you will be justified by them or you will be condemned.*
The words we speak during our life can condemn us or justify us on Judgment Day.

What kinds of words should I speak?

Deuteronomy 6:4-7 *You must commit yourselves wholeheartedly to these commands I am giving you today. Repeat them again and again to your children. Talk about them when you are at home and when you are away on a journey, when you are lying down and when you are getting up again.*
Talk about God's commands on a continual basis.

Job 16:5 *I would speak in a way that helps you. I would try to take away your grief.*

Ephesians 4:29 *Let everything you say be good and helpful, so that your words will be an encouragement to those who hear them.*
Try to help others and build them up with what you say.

Psalm 50:23 *Giving thanks is a sacrifice that truly honors me.*
Speak words of thanks and praise to God.

Proverbs 25:11 *Timely advice is as lovely as golden apples in a silver basket.*
When the time is right, giving good advice can be very beneficial.

PROMISE FROM GOD: Proverbs 10:20 *The words of the godly are like sterling silver.*

Proverbs 12:13 *The wicked are trapped by their own words, but the godly escape such trouble.*

WORK

Does God care what kind of work I do?
Ecclesiastes 12:14 *God will judge us for everything we do, including every secret thing, whether good or bad.*
God cares about what we do and how well we do it.

1 Kings 11:28 *Jeroboam was a very capable young man, and when Solomon saw how industrious he was, he put him in charge of the labor force from the tribes of Ephraim and Manasseh.*

Ecclesiastes 9:10 *Whatever you do, do well.* We should be industrious and do the best work we can.

Proverbs 13:11 *Wealth from get-rich-quick schemes quickly disappears; wealth from hard work grows.*
Honest, hard work is much better than schemes to get rich quickly.

Proverbs 26:13-16 *The lazy person is full of excuses, saying, "I can't go outside because there might be a lion on the road! Yes, I'm sure there's a lion out there!" As a door turns back and forth on its hinges, so the lazy person turns over in bed. Some people are so lazy that they won't lift a finger to feed themselves. Lazy people consider themselves smarter than seven wise counselors.*

2 Thessalonians 3:11-12 *We hear that some of you are living idle lives, refusing to work and wasting time meddling in other people's business. In the name of the Lord Jesus Christ, we appeal to such people—no, we command them: Settle down and get to work. Earn your own living.*
Instead of finding excuses not to work, we should work hard.

What attitude should I have toward my work?

Romans 12:11 *Never be lazy in your work, but serve the Lord enthusiastically.*

Ephesians 6:6-7 *Work hard, but not just to please your masters when they are watching. As slaves of Christ, do the will of God with all your heart. Work with enthusiasm, as though you were working for the Lord rather than for people.*

We should work with enthusiasm at whatever we do, keeping in mind that we are serving God, not people.

1 Thessalonians 4:11-12 *This should be your ambition: to live a quiet life, minding your own business and working with your hands. . . . As a result, people who are not Christians will respect the way you live, and you will not need to depend on others to meet your financial needs.*

Our attitude toward work should include the goal of honoring God by the way we work and support ourselves.

James 3:13 *If you are wise and understand God's ways, live a life of steady goodness so that only good deeds will pour forth. And if you don't brag about the good you do, then you will be truly wise!*

God wants us to steadily do good work with an attitude of humility, rather than continually pointing at our own accomplishments.

PROMISE FROM GOD: Proverbs
1 0 : 4 *Lazy people are soon poor; hard workers get rich.*

Proverbs 1 2 : 1 1 *Hard work means prosperity; only fools idle away their time.*

WORRY

When does worry become sin?

Matthew 1 3 : 2 2 *The thorny ground represents those who hear and accept the Good News, but all too quickly the message is crowded out by the cares of this life.*

Colossians 3 : 2 *Let heaven fill your thoughts. Do not think only about things down here on earth.* Our worry over the concerns of life becomes sin when it prevents the word of God from taking root in our lives.

Why do I worry so much? How can I worry less?

Psalm 5 5 : 1 - 5 *My heart is in anguish.* Fear and anxiety are normal responses to threatening situations.

Exodus 1 4 : 1 3 *Moses told the people, "Don't be afraid. Just stand where you are and watch the LORD rescue you."* We combat worry and anxiety by remembering and trusting God's promises.

Philippians 4:6 *Don't worry about anything; instead, pray about everything.*
We combat worry by placing our cares in Jesus' hands.

Psalm 62:6 *He alone is my rock and my salvation, my fortress where I will not be shaken.*
We find relief from fear in the promise of salvation.

Matthew 6:27 *Can all your worries add a single moment to your life?*
Our worries lose their grip on us as we focus on Kingdom priorities.

PROMISE FROM GOD: 1 Peter 5:7 *Give all your worries and cares to God, for he cares about what happens to you.*

WORSHIP

Why is worship an important part of our relationship with God?

2 Kings 17:36 *Worship only the LORD, who brought you out of Egypt with such mighty miracles and power.*

1 Chronicles 16:29 *Give to the LORD the glory he deserves! . . . Worship the LORD in all his holy splendor.*

Worship is the recognition of who God is, and of who we are in relation to him.

Exodus 29:43 *I will meet the people of Israel there, and the Tabernacle will be sanctified by my glorious presence.*
God meets with his people in a powerful way when they worship him together.

Deuteronomy 31:11 *You must read this law to all the people of Israel when they assemble before the LORD your God at the place he chooses.*

Micah 4:2 *Come, let us go up to the mountain of the LORD, to the Temple of the God of Israel. There he will teach us his ways, so that we may obey him.*
Public, corporate worship gives God's people an important opportunity to hear his word proclaimed and learn about God and his ways.

Psalm 5:7 *Because of your unfailing love, I can enter your house; with deepest awe I will worship at your Temple.*

Psalm 100:1-3 *Shout with joy to the LORD, O earth! Worship the LORD with gladness. Come before him, singing with joy. Acknowledge that the LORD is God! He made us, and we are his.*

Isaiah 6:3 *In a great chorus they sang, "Holy, holy, holy is the LORD Almighty! The whole earth is filled with his glory!"*

Worship is a fitting response to God's holiness, power, and grace.

Revelation 5:11-12 *I looked again, and I heard the singing of thousands and millions of angels around the throne and the living beings and the elders. And they sang in a mighty chorus: "The Lamb is worthy—the Lamb who was killed. He is worthy to receive power and riches and wisdom and strength and honor and glory and blessing."*
Our worship of God is a foretaste of heaven.

What are some principles to guide us in our worship?

Deuteronomy 11:16 *Do not let your heart turn away from the LORD to worship other gods.*

Revelation 22:9 *Again he said, "No, don't worship me. I am a servant of God. . . . Worship God!"*
We must worship only God.

Exodus 3:5 *"Do not come any closer," God told him. "Take off your sandals, for you are standing on holy ground."*
When we enter God's presence in worship, we should recognize that we are on holy ground.

Psalm 35:18 *I will thank you in front of the entire congregation. I will praise you before all the people.*

318

Hebrews 13:15 *With Jesus' help, let us continually offer our sacrifice of praise to God by proclaiming the glory of his name.*
Our worship should include praise and giving thanks to God for what he has done.

Psalm 30:4 *Sing to the LORD, all you godly ones!*

Ephesians 5:19 *Then you will sing psalms and hymns and spiritual songs among yourselves, making music to the Lord in your hearts.*
Singing is an important part of our worship to God.

Psalm 33:2 *Praise the LORD with melodies on the lyre; make music for him on the ten-stringed harp.*

Psalm 150:3-5 *Praise him with a blast of the trumpet; praise him with the lyre and harp! Praise him with the tambourine and dancing; praise him with stringed instruments and flutes! Praise him with a clash of cymbals; praise him with loud clanging cymbals.*
Musical instruments can have an important role to play in our worship.

Deuteronomy 31:12 *Call them all together—men, women, children, and the foreigners living in your towns—so they may listen and learn to fear the LORD your God.*

2 Chronicles 20:13 *All the men of Judah stood before the LORD with their little ones, wives, and children.*
It is good for everyone in the family to be together for corporate worship.

1 Chronicles 15:16 *David also ordered the Levite leaders to appoint a choir of Levites who were singers and musicians to sing joyful songs to the accompaniment of lyres, harps, and cymbals.*
A choir can aid in worship.

Psalm 95:6 *Come, let us worship and bow down. Let us kneel before the LORD our maker.*
Kneeling and bowing are appropriate postures for worship.

Hebrews 12:28 *Since we are receiving a Kingdom that cannot be destroyed, let us be thankful and please God by worshiping him with holy fear and awe.*
Holy fear and awe should be our attitude in worship.

John 4:23-24 *God is Spirit, so those who worship him must worship in spirit and in truth.*
Worship must be in spirit and in truth.

1 Corinthians 11:23-25 *On the night when he was betrayed, the Lord Jesus took a loaf of bread, and when he had given thanks, he broke it and said, "This is my body, which is given for you. Do this in remembrance of me." In the same way, he took the*

cup of wine after supper, saying, "This cup is the new covenant between God and you, sealed by the shedding of my blood. Do this in remembrance of me as often as you drink it."

The Lord's supper is both an act of worship to God and an act of fellowship among believers.

1 Corinthians 14:26 *When you meet, one will sing, another will teach, another will tell some special revelation God has given, one will speak in an unknown language, while another will interpret what is said. But everything that is done must be useful to all and build them up in the Lord.*

Everyone has something valuable to contribute to public worship, but all things must be done properly and in order.

PROMISE FROM GOD: Isaiah 35:10 *Those who have been ransomed by the LORD will return to Jerusalem, singing songs of everlasting joy. Sorrow and mourning will disappear, and they will be overcome with joy and gladness.*

INDEX